The Daily Telegraph

STARTING
& RUNNING
A B&B

If you want to know how...

Starting Your Own Business
*The best-selling guide to planning
and building a successful enterprise*

Starting & Running a B&B in France
*How to make money and enjoy a new lifestyle running
your own chambres d'hôte*

Going for Self-Employment
How to set up and run your own business

Book-keeping & Accounting for the Small Business
*How to keep the books and maintain financial
control over your business*

How To Books
3 Newtec Place, Magdalen Road,
Oxford OX4 1RE, United Kingdom
E-mail: info@howtobooks.co.uk
http://www.howtobooks.co.uk

The Daily Telegraph

Starting &
Running
a B&B

A practical guide to setting up and managing
a Bed and Breakfast business

Stewart Whyte

in consultation with Nigel Jess

howtobooks

Published by How To Books Ltd,
3 Newtec Place, Magdalen Road,
Oxford OX4 1RE. United Kingdom.
Tel: (01865) 793806. Fax: (01865) 248780.
email: info@howtobooks.co.uk
http://www.howtobooks.co.uk

First edition 2003
Reprinted 2003
Reprinted 2004 (twice)
Reprinted 2005

British Library Cataloguing in Publication Data
A catalogue record for this book is available from the British Library

Cover design by Baseline Arts Ltd, Oxford
Produced for How To Books by Deer Park Productions
Illustrations by Nicki Averill
Typeset by PDQ Typesetting, Newcastle-under-Lyme, Staffs.
Printed and bound in Great Britain by Bell & Bain Ltd., Glasgow

NOTE: The material contained in this book is set out in good faith for general guidance and no liability
can be accepted for loss or expense incurred as a result of relying in particular circumstances on
statements made in the book. The laws and regulations are complex and liable to change, and readers
should check the current position with the relevant authorities before making personal arrangements.

ISBN: 1 85703 883 5

Contents

Part Two: How To Run Your B&B Efficiently and Successfully

To invite someone to be our guest
Is to undertake responsibility for
Their happiness all the time that
They are under our roof.

Jean Anthelme Brillat-Savarin (1755–1826)
Author, epicure, raconteur

Thank you for buying one of our books. We hope you'll enjoy this book, and that it will help you start and run your own successful **B&B** business.

We always try to ensure our books are up to date, but contact details seem to change so quickly that it can be very hard to keep up with them. If you do have any problems contacting any of the organisations listed at the back of the book please get in touch, and either we or the author will do what we can to help. And if you do find correct contact details that differ from those in the book, please let us know so that we can put it right when we reprint.

Please also give us your feedback so we can go on making books that you want to read. If there's anything you particularly liked about this book – or you have suggestions about how it could be improved in the future – email us on info@howtobooks.co.uk

Good luck with your new venture, we hope you enjoy your new lifestyle and that your **B&B** is a great success.

The Publishers
www.howtobooks.co.uk

Preface

The growth of Bed and Breakfast as an accommodation alternative is a success story unparalleled throughout the Western world and, in particular, the United Kingdom and Ireland. To meet demand and substantiate Bed and Breakfast's place in the tourism industry there is now a growing need for increased knowledge and professionalism among Bed and Breakfast operators. Far too many are catering for the lower end of the market when more establishments should be providing better facilities and service for the ever-growing numbers of discerning and affluent travellers.

Participation in tourism can be an exciting lifestyle venture, especially in the Bed and Breakfast industry. It is relatively easy to enter and has the potential to be both financially and personally rewarding. The traditional Bed and Breakfast is a privately owned premises that offers value for money, accommodation inclusive of breakfast, quaintness and hospitality, and opportunities for the guest to exchange ideas with the host and be the recipient of sound, local, sightseeing advice. In the main, the traditional B&B is a home where both the host and his or her guests are sheltered under the same roof.

The above definition applies to small hotels, some pubs, and guesthouses that have no more than eight serviced bedrooms and is current throughout the United Kingdom, Ireland, the Channel Islands and the Isle of Man. The six bedspace rule may apply.

The conceptional focus, however, is placed on the personal interaction and assistance the host provides to the guest and not just the bricks and mortar content. This is what forms the true intrinsic value of Bed and Breakfast accommodation.

As aside from the interest in entering the market as a proprietor, there is increasing interest by the public in staying in B&Bs while touring, or as a viable short break holiday option. With this rise in popularity, however, come expectations and this is what is discussed in this book.

Current trends show that changes in the workplace could be one of the main contributors to the high level of interest in becoming a Bed & Breakfast operator. Another influential factor is the growth of the short break holiday market. Those who take short break holidays historically prefer this form of accommodation.

It is important to remember, however, that knowledge is not an end in itself. You must use the knowledge gained from this publication as a resource and stepping stone to achieve your goals and aspirations. The main message is that the research you need to do to make your B&B a success must be personal to you and your market.

Starting & Running a B & B – A practical guide to setting up and managing a Bed and Breakfast business, has been assembled by a team of experienced researchers and operators who have carefully studied the practicalities and the needs of people who are either in the industry or wish to enter it. In constructing the book we have tried to avoid duplication of material that exists in other training manuals and how-to publications, preferring to concentrate on that which is directly applicable to the industry. We have gathered up-to-date information from industry leaders and practitioners, both nationally and inter-nationally, to give the reader a source of information, which reflects the practicalities and requirements necessary for the successful Bed and Breakfast operator.

All of these issues are significant, but professionalism is the most important. This book will reinforce the need to seek professional advice in the early stage of your venture and give you an insight into the level of professionalism you need to consider in order to be a success in this business.

Good luck on your venture!

Stewart Whyte

Acknowledgements

This book would not be as comprehensive without the wonderful contribution of the following people and organisations:

Dr Rita Helling for her comments on Linguistic Programming; Gideon & Sara Stanley from Gracesoft; Paul Ricardo for his Internet advice; Sealy of UK; English Tourism Council & Star UK, Northern Ireland Tourist Board, Bord Fáilte, Department of Tourism & Leisure – Isle of Man and Jersey & Guernsey Tourism regarding tourism research statistics; also Abergavenny, Exeter, Windermere, Keswick, Stamford and Worcester Tourist Offices; the Scottish Tourist Offices and Colin Houston from VisitScotland; Wales Tourist Board for their helpful insights; Northern Ireland Farm & Country Holidays Association; N.I. Bed & Breakfast Association; The Town & Country Homes Assoc'n (Bed & Breakfast Ireland); Wrightlines; The Irish Farmhouse Holidays Association (Fáilte Tuaithe), Bed & Breakfast (UK) Ltd; AA Hotel Services – Lifestyle Guides, Jacqueline Elmslie; Max Mosher and Energy Saving Trust for their advice on energy saving considerations; Warren Whyte, General Manager of Custom House Currency Exchange for his advice on banking procedures; Sue & John Armstrong from Appletrees B&B for their overall suggestions on running a B&B, to Patricia from Halcyon B&B, Paula and Neil from Abbingdon B&B, James and Olive from Cullenta House, Margaret from Loyola B&B, Anne and Robin from Harbour Heights, Judith from Kynance Bay House and Jennifer and Brian who introduced Suellen to Judith and for their hospitality; Matthew Welch (Partner) Fisher Jones Greenwood, Solicitors London and William Fry, Solicitors Dublin for their respective advice on alcohol licensing; a special thanks to Helen and Warren from Stamford, Elizabeth and Nigel from Banbridge, and Dee and Charles from Worcester for their hospitality.

I would also like to thank Jo & Graham Moule of Mount Tavy Cottage Bed & Breakfast, in Tavistock (www.mounttavy.freeserve co.uk) for the photographs used on our front cover.

This book is easy to read due to the editing expertise of Suellen Harwood. Her research skills and ability to expand the text is greatly appreciated. For this I thank her.

I would like to thank all of the Bed & Breakfast owners for their advice and tips which will prove invaluable to all the newcomers in the industry.

Until next time,
Stewart

Introduction

Starting & Running a B & B – A practical guide to setting up and managing a Bed and Breakfast business is divided into two main sections for easy access. The first section (Chapters 1–5) is designed for you to discover if you, your partner and family, your home and your bank balance are ready to enter this industry. It will also help you to decide what level of commitment you are prepared to make to this venture: full-time/weekends/breakfasts only/full board, etc.

If you have decided that operating a Bed and Breakfast is your dream for a better future then the second section (Chapters 6–13) will be an introduction to the daily issues that confront Bed and Breakfast operators, and will outline how to run a Bed and Breakfast efficiently and successfully.

Throughout this book you will find two symbols. The single symbol 🏠 is applicable to all operators, but in particular to those whose commitment to the enterprise is on a very small scale (perhaps one or two bedrooms, and not the only source of income). The double symbol 🏠 🏠 is for those whose enterprise will run on a larger scale and who need it to contribute substantially to the household income.

The following are questions you might like to ask yourself before you read any further. As you progress through the book you may like to return to this page to see how your ideas on what it takes to run a successful Bed and Breakfast have altered.

♦ What parts of my character make me a perfect host or hostess?
♦ What implications do I think that owning and operating a Bed and Breakfast will have on my personal life?

- Who will be my target market?

- What facilities do I already have?

- What additional facilities do I think I will need to provide or acquire?

- What financial investment do I think will be needed to start the venture?

- Do I have this amount available?

- If not, where do I expect it will come from?

- Who do I expect to be my customers?

- Why will they come to my Bed and Breakfast rather than some other type of accommodation?

- How will my potential customers hear about my Bed and Breakfast?

- Will I advertise? If so, where will I advertise?

- How much do I intend to charge?

- What factors did I look at to reach this figure?

- What factors will influence whether my establishment makes a profit or loss?

- What legal obligations do I have?

- What are the main skills needed to run a successful Bed and Breakfast business?

- What are my main skills?

- What kinds of additional help will I require?

- Where will this help come from?

- How much do I know about employing people?

- When do I intend to begin accommodating guests?

- What factors are most likely to inhibit me?

- What will my feasibility study contain and does it make sense?

Having taken stock of your current expectations and knowledge, we will begin looking into the who, what, why and wherefores of operating a successful Bed and Breakfast in the United Kingdom, Ireland, the Channel Islands and the Isle of Man.

Part One

Preparing to Enter the B&B Business

1
It's Up To You

S o, you want to run a Bed & Breakfast! *Why?* This is very possibly the most important question you will ask yourself as you read this book.

Why? Is it because you have stayed in a few B&Bs over the years and it seems such a nice way to earn a living? Is it because you went away for the weekend and saw this gorgeous period or historic house and it was only £350,000 or €200,000 and it would be such fun to do up, and hadn't you both talked about making a *sea change* decision and moving out of the city? Is it because you really like to cook, and have always loved it when your best friend and her family visit you from distant places? Is it because you think it will be a way to make your fortune?

There are many different reasons why people enter the Bed & Breakfast market and you need to think clearly about why it is that you wish to enter it. Because, make no mistake about it, the difference between a good and bad B&B is you, the host. Why you are embarking on this adventure matters, because you need to create a business plan that will match the goals you have for your Bed & Breakfast. Be prepared to discover that running a B&B may not achieve those goals for you.

TIP

Be prepared to roll up your
sleeves past your elbows!

The harsh news is that very few B&Bs will support you in the first few years. First things first: if you start with two guest bedrooms your earning capacity will be limited.

The main reasons for failure are over-capitalising on the part of the owners, and the management process of the property itself. Burnout can also be a significant factor in the pursuit of a lifestyle change.

There is a difference in spending on essentials, such as en suites in each guest bedroom, which are rapidly becoming a necessity, and filling your house with expensive antiques which will not always make a guest decide to stay with you, or to return.

A flair for redecorating does not necessarily make you a good host. Neither does enjoying entertaining friends and family. Running a Bed & Breakfast is a 24-hour commitment. You need to be prepared to 'entertain' at all hours of the day and night, have your private life disturbed, and in some cases share your personal space with strangers. This is difficult, but if you are to be a successful host the spirit of giving must be embraced 24 hours a day. This spirit should inhabit every exchange, every phone call, every letter or email. To be a successful host you need to *love people* and be prepared to share your life and home with them. But, never forget you need quality time for yourself and your family.

TIP

Identify your target market prior
to deciding whether your family
is ready and your property is
suitable.

IT'S ALL ABOUT PERSONALITY

As you work through this book you are going to be asked a lot of questions. Now is the time to start a notebook to record the answers to all the questions asked of you. This will be invaluable in determining your market and creating your feasibility study. At the same time start a folder for filing all the information you will need to collect prior to starting your B&B.

♦ Do you have the type of personality that will make you a wonderful host? Write down your answers and refer to them later when evaluating whether you are the right kind of person to run a Bed & Breakfast.

♦ Do you like people? This is very important. You can't just think that people are OK when you enter the B&B industry. You need to genuinely like people and be interested in them. You have to love individuals and the idiosyncrasies that come with individualism.

♦ Are you prepared to do almost anything to make your guests feel important and spoiled? This is the essence of a good host.

♦ Will you enjoy guests, who are in effect strangers, wandering in and out of your home, treating it as if it were their own? When you are living in the same house as your guests, privacy will become a thing of the past.

♦ Are you willing to be available 24 hours a day? Guests and potential guests have the habit of calling, arriving or wanting your help at the most inopportune times. You need to be prepared to drop whatever it is you are doing and provide service with a smile.

♦ Are you going to be able to live with a difficult person over the whole time of their visit? And will you be able to cope with this person in your home? People can be difficult and if you don't have the patience of a saint you may find this life hard.

- Can you accept the old adage that the customer is always right? Guests, or potential guests, may be demanding and want things that are unreasonable. Some of their needs will be impossible, however you must be prepared to compromise and try to make your guest happy whenever possible, even when it's against your better judgement. You can't afford to be Basil Fawlty! Word of mouth is the key here, use it as a marketing tool. Your guests' stay should be of such high quality that they act as your ambassadors, spreading the good news of your B&B.

> **TIP**
>
> If you can't find it in your heart to make a grumpy person smile, keep out of the people business.

- Are your partner and family as equally committed to this lifestyle choice as you are? Without passion on all sides you are destined for failure, early burnout, or at worst, relationship difficulties.

- Are you a dedicated housekeeper? Untidiness just won't do as a Bed & Breakfast operator. You need to be a fastidious housekeeper. Do you enjoy vacuuming every day? Do you notice if something is out of place? Do your friends call you a perfectionist? Good. These are the perfect qualities for a B&B host, where near enough is never good enough.

THE DREAM OF WORKING FOR YOURSELF

Being your own boss can be a great way to earn a living. Most of us have had this dream. Being able to throw your job in and to strike out on your own. Make your mark. Keep the profits for yourself. And for many that is where it stays – a dream. However, a few of us decide to take the plunge and whether or not we are successful in our endeavour primarily depends on two things: our motivation for entering a business to begin with, and our preparedness for entering that business at that time.

Successful small business operators have chosen to work for themselves for positive reasons. Not because they hate what they are leaving behind, but because they are excited about creating something for the future – including profits.

They often are extremely motivated and self-disciplined. Not only does your goal need to be uppermost in your mind when opening your own business, you must have the discipline to divide work from your private life – particularly when your business is in your home. Successful small business people thrive away from the constraints of an employer.

Financial goals are also an important focus for the successful small business owner. Your business plan needs to clearly set out the financial goals for your business with strategies to help you reach them. The most successful small business people have a financial and career goal that cannot be satisfied by working for someone else.

You also need to realise you are leaving the world of the secure pay packet. Gone forever are the hidden financial benefits of working for a wage or salary. It is now all up to you. You need to feel comfortable about this and should consider consulting a financial planner for advice about managing your financial future.

THE FINANCIAL REALITY

The bad news is that most small businesses fail during the first three years. The main reason for this is lack of planning by the owner, both at the set-up stage and ongoing.

Entering the ranks for the wrong reason to begin with exacerbates this.

The worst reasons to go into business for yourself are: that no one else will employ you; you want flexible working hours, that is more time to play than work; and you think that all it takes to make a fortune in your own business is a good idea. This last statement is the biggest misconception.

The best ideas in the world won't work if you don't plan to succeed – and have the ability to convince everyone else that your idea *is* a good idea.

The reasons most often cited for failure in small businesses are:

◆ A lack of business and/or management experience.
◆ Inadequate, inaccurate or non-existent financial records.
◆ Taking too much money from the business for personal use.
◆ Lack of adequate seed capital.

A solid **business plan** will help prevent you becoming another statistic. We all know about the bottom line, but the top line, that is research, is equally important. Thorough research in the early stages of your venture makes you less likely to fail in the long run.

Consider both the advantages and disadvantages of being your own boss. There is no doubt that it will place some stresses on your lifestyle and relationships in the first few years while you establish a pattern.

Bonuses can be self-satisfaction, management autonomy and building financial independence. Negatives can be sporadic income, long and irregular hours, competition, possible failure, and relationship difficulties.

MONEY IN THE BANK

Unless you are going into Bed & Breakfast as a hobby or interest, money could be a problem for the first few years.

Many B&B operators make the mistake that holidaymakers are just waiting for them to open their doors and then they will be booked up for months. This doesn't always happen. B&Bs, for the most part, are built on word of mouth and word of mouth takes time to spread.

You need to have a plan on how you will financially survive until you build a clientele.

+ How much money do you have in the bank?

+ How long can you survive with your outgoings outweighing your income?

+ Do you fully own your property (this being the most comfortable financial option)?

+ Do you or your partner plan to supplement your income with a second job?

Think about these questions and try to put together a **financial contingency plan** allowing for a slow flow of guests at first.

A LOOK IN THE MIRROR

Before we go any further take a look in the mirror. Hard. Then ask yourself the following questions. An *honest* answer to these questions will help you decide whether you are the right person to enter the B&B market and will help to reduce the potential for failure.

- Are you self-driven? When you work for yourself you need to be able to motivate yourself.

- Are you organised? Running a business by yourself or with a partner, needs systematic planning.

- Do both you and your partner share the right temperament to be a B&B host? Are you both friendly, relaxed, organised and charming?

- Are you a problem-solver or do you tend to become indecisive when faced with a lot of problems or questions? Running a business requires constant decision-making and the ability to prevent a crisis.

- Are you confident, without being overbearing? You need to be able to sell your business to banks, customers, the media, etc. The essence of a good B&B operator, however, is warmth of personality, you need to have the ability to attract people to you, not distance them from you.

- Are you willing to take advice and learn from others? Successful business people are always on the lookout for good ideas and advice. They then take the best of this and mould it into their business. They work *on* their business not *in* it.

- Are you prepared to learn the skills needed to run a business? This takes time and effort.

◆ Are you experienced in leading people, and are you prepared to learn? Owning a business often requires you to hire, motivate, and in the worst cases, dismiss staff. This takes a certain skill.

◆ Have you the ability to set clear and attainable goals? You need a business plan that is achievable, otherwise you are setting yourself up for disappointment.

◆ Have you skills of negotiation? Owning your own business will require the forming of relationships with other business people around you. In times of conflict, you need to be able to negotiate win-win agreements with all the parties concerned.

◆ Can you handle stress? If heavy traffic or queues worry you, this is nothing to the stress you may experience when you have a cash flow problem – an all too common problem when operating a small business.

◆ Do you have strong communication skills? Being a host requires the attributes of a perfect personality. You need to be naturally pleasant and agreeable. Those of you who are moody will probably not find this way of life to your liking. You need to be able to make conversation while avoiding political or religious topics, or other discussion minefields. You need to be patient and tolerant and know the difference between making polite conversation and becoming a nuisance.

A FAMILY AFFAIR

Operating a Bed & Breakfast with a family means that not only should you have the right personality for hosting guests, but so should the other members of your family. Success in Bed & Breakfast is dependent on an equal commitment from everybody concerned.

TIP

Before going into the business of Bed & Breakfast stay in a few yourself so you better understand what the host has to cope with.

Living on the premises of your business can be distracting enough for an individual – for those of you with a family this disruption can be ten-fold. It is not impossible for you to run both a successful B&B and raise a family on the same premises, but it does require family co-operation and understanding.

You should factor into your business plan contingencies that should ensure the success of your business without disrupting your family's happiness. You might want to consider the following.

◆ Having a defined letting period to protect your family's privacy. For example, and depending on the tourist authority you are operating under, you might only let rooms four nights a week or 40 weeks a year, taking your break in the low season. This limitation will, however, affect your income projections, so you must factor this into your business plan.

◆ Consider having a separate annex for your family so that family life is separated from your business life.

◆ Organise time out for you and your family to spend time away from your 'office'. No one wants to spend 365 days a year, 24 hours a day at their workplace. If you have children living at home then three nights and four days of having guests may be the maximum (again check with the tourist authority you are under that this is feasible) – if you want to retain family unity.

◆ Have a friend or colleague who can be available to step in and act as a paid caretaker of your business should you need to get away, or if you are unwell.

◆ Factor in time to discuss and explain to your children why you are entering this business and what the consequences may be for them.

Their co-operation will be directly proportional to their level of understanding.

♦ Explain to your children that they are to be polite and friendly to guests at all times, and not to impose on them unless asked. Remember many couples who frequent B&Bs come to escape their children – they won't want to spend time with yours.

♦ If your children are very young, you should really consider whether now is the right time for you to open your B&B. Both raising very young children and running a B&B are physically and emotionally draining. Trying to juggle both could see you lose your sense of balance.

The other consideration of running a B&B with children at home is that they will want to spend time with you when they are at home, which is primarily at weekends. Weekends, however, are often your busiest trading period. You will need to balance these two claims on your time.

> **TIP**
>
> Be mindful of the impact Bed & Breakfast has on family life, especially if your children still live at home. Life as you know it will never be the same.

Equal commitment within your family structure is crucial. Tension between family members becomes palpable and your guests will feel it. This will be uncomfortable for all concerned and will not result in return visits.

GOING IT ALONE

Is it possible to do this without a family? It certainly is – more and more Bed & Breakfasts are being run by single people. In some ways you may find this way of life easier than those with a family or an uncommitted partner, as you know you are committed to your business and will ensure that everything is as it should be.

The only disadvantages are time out periods – which you will need if you are to be successful. Ensure that you have time out from the business to do other things you enjoy. If you have always wanted to do drawing classes, do it. If you want to go on holidays think of hiring an experienced couple to mind your operation while you are away – there are a number of professionals who specialise in this. Have your phone calls linked to your mobile and participate in life.

TIP

One of the nice things about Bed & Breakfast is the flexibility of being able to decide when to have guests.

The other thing is not to over-host your guests – or use them to stave off loneliness. As a good B&B host you should know when your guests want your company and when they do not. This is where your people skills will come in.

IT'S TIME

So you are comfortable that you have the right personality to make a success of the Bed & Breakfast business.

It's now time to get a better appreciation of the tourist trends as they apply to your country. This is important information to know because it can influence future decisions.

2

Who Is Your Market?

B efore deciding exactly whom you are going to target for your Bed & Breakfast, it is a good idea to know something about tourism in your country. The following statistics were obtained from the following sources:

- ◆ Star UK, sponsored by the national tourist boards of England, Northern Ireland, Scotland, Wales and the Department for Culture Media and Sport.
- ◆ Bord Fáilte – Tourism Facts 2003.
- ◆ Northern Ireland Tourist Board.

INTERNATIONAL MARKET

Tourism is one of the largest industries in the United Kingdom, Ireland, the Channel Islands and the Isle of Man. As a guide there are listed below, in table form, the base 2001-year indicators, which will enable you to better understand who your market is.

Wales

Volume and tourist spending in Wales

	Trips/visits (millions)	Nights (millions)	Spending (£ millions)
UK residents	11.9	39.8	1,543
Overseas residents	0.9	6.6	252

Purpose of visit to Wales

	UK residents trips (millions)	Spending (£ millions)	Overseas residents visits (millions)	Spending (£ millions)
Holiday	8.8	1,196	0.29	73
Visiting friends or relatives	1.0	166	0.15	56
Business	1.9	166	0.31	84
Other	0.2	13	0.11	40
All purposes	11.9	1,543	0.90	252

Holidays in Wales

Nights	UK residents trips (millions)	Nights (millions)	Spending (£ millions)	Overseas residents visits (millions)	Nights (millions)	Spending (£ millions)
1-3	5.3	10.4	582	0.07	0.11	6
4-7	2.9	15.3	496	0.11	0.39	8
8+	0.6	6.4	119	0.19	1.29	51
Total holidays	8.8	32.1	1,196	0.37	1.79	75

Note: Overseas figures represent 2001

Seasonality of tourism in Wales

	UK residents % of trips	Overseas residents % of visits
Jan, Feb, Mar	19	14
Apr, May, Jun	27	30
Jul, Aug, Sept	34	40
Oct, Nov, Dec	20	16

Accommodation used in Wales

	Trips %	UK residents spending %
Hotel/motel/guesthouse	18	29
B&B/farmhouse/flat/chalet	7	8
Rented house/flat/chalet	6	10
Hostel/university/school	1	1
Friends/relatives' home	35	24
Second home/timeshare	3	1
Camping	4	3
Towed caravan	8	6
Static caravan (owned)	8	5
Other	12	13

Accommodation used by overseas residents

	Visits %	Overseas residents spending %
Hotel etc	34	32
B&B	14	11
Camping/mobile home	5	4
Hostel	4	6
Holiday village/centre	0	0
Rented house	2	7
Paying guest	0	1
Free guest	37	37
Own home	1	1
Other	4	1

Scotland

Volume and tourist spending in Scotland

	Trips/visits (millions)	Nights (millions)	Spending (£ millions)
UK residents	1.85	64.5	3,682
Overseas residents	1.58	15.0	806

Purpose of visit to Scotland

	UK residents trips (millions)	Spending (£ millions)	Overseas residents visits (millions)	Spending (£ millions)
Holiday	12	2,469	0.83	411
Visiting friends or relatives	2.8	389	0.27	144
Business	3.3	331	0.41	192
Other	0.4	43	0.08	59
All purposes	185	3,682	1.58	800

Holidays in Scotland

Nights	UK residents trips (millions)	Nights (millions)	Spending (£ millions)	Overseas residents visits (millions)	Nights (millions)	Spending (£ millions)
1–3	7.0	13.9	1,173	0.07	0.2	21
4–7	3.6	18.8	907	0.20	0.9	76
8+	1.3	13.3	389	0.51	4.9	254
Total holidays	12.0	46.1	2,469	0.78	6.0	351

Note: Overseas Residents represent 2001 figures

Seasonality of tourism in Scotland

	UK residents % of trips	Overseas residents % of visits
Jan, Feb, Mar	21	11
Apr, May, Jun	25	24
Jul, Aug, Sept	29	51
Oct, Nov, Dec	25	14

Accommodation used in Scotland

	Trips %	UK residents spending %
Hotel/motel/guesthouse	32	43
B&B/farmhouse	8	10
Rented house/flat/chalet	5	7
Hostel/university/school	1	1
Friends/relatives' home	42	24
Second home/timeshare	2	4
Camping	2	1
Towed caravan	1	1
Other	10	9

Accommodation used by overseas residents

	Visits %	Overseas residents spending %
Hotel etc	45	43
B&B	17	12
Camping/mobile home	4	2
Hostel	8	6
Holiday village/centre	0	0
Rented house	4	7
Paying guest	1	1
Free guest	28	24
Own home	2	4
Other	2	2

England

Volume and tourist spending in England

	Trips/visits (millions)	Nights (millions)	Spending (£ millions)
UK residents	134	415.8	20,778
Overseas residents	20.5	175.3	10,313

Purpose of visit to England

	UK residents trips (millions)	Spending (£ millions)	Overseas residents visits (millions)	Spending (£ millions)
Holiday	79.8	13,252	6.7	3,098
Visiting friends or relatives	33.7	2,810	5.8	2,210
Business	19.1	4,416	5.6	3,276
Other	2.2	309	2.4	1,730
All purposes	1349	20,778	20.5	10,313

Holidays in England

Nights	UK residents trips (millions)	Nights (millions)	Spending (£ millions)	Overseas residents visits (millions)	Nights (millions)	Spending (£ millions)
1–3	57.2	97.9	6,778	2.50	5.7	611
4–7	22.1	117.0	4,812	2.35	11.8	949
8+	6.4	66.0	1,662	1.72	28.7	1,323
Total holidays	79.8	280.9	13,252	6.57	46.2	2,883

Note: Overseas Residents represent 2001 figures

Seasonality of tourism in England

	UK residents % of trips	Overseas residents % of visits
Jan, Feb, Mar	21	19
Apr, May, Jun	26	26
Jul, Aug, Sept	29	30
Oct, Nov, Dec	24	24

Accommodation used in England

	Trips %	UK residents spending %
Hotel/motel/guesthouse	26	40
B&B/farmhouse	6	7
Rented house/flat/chalet	6	9
Hostel/university/school	1	1
Friends/relatives' home	48	28
Second home/timeshare	1	1
Camping	2	1
Towed caravan	3	2
Other	9	11

Accommodation used by overseas residents

	Visits %	Overseas residents spending %
Hotel etc	45	47
B&B	4	3
Camping/mobile home	1	0
Hostel	4	6
Holiday village/centre	0	0
Rented house	2	7
Paying guest	3	4
Free guest	39	28
Own home	2	3
Other	5	1

Northern Ireland

Volume and tourist spending of tourists

	Trips/visits (millions)	Nights (millions)	Spending (£ millions)
Tourists	17.4	8.56	274

Seasonality of Tourism 2002

	%
Jan, Feb, Mar	20
Apr, May, Jun	25
Jul, Aug, Sept	32
Oct, Nov, Dec	23

Where did they stay in Northern Ireland

	Visits %	Spending %
Hotel	29	35
Guesthouse/Bed & Breakfast	9	10
Caravan/Camping	1	1
Rented Accommodation	2	6
Staying with friends/relatives	55	44
Other	4	4

Sources: Northern Ireland Passenger Survey

Weekend/weekday occupancy comparisons by region 2001

Region	Weekday % room	Weekend % room
Belfast	38	49
North West	20	19
North East	32	25
South West	24	19
South East	25	27

The Republic of Ireland

Volume and tourist spending in the Republic of Ireland 2003

	Trips/visits (millions)	Spending € (millions)
UK residents	3,553	1,319
Northern Ireland	596	178
Total out of state	6,774	3,406

Purpose of visit to the Republic of Ireland 2003

	Total %	Britain %	Mainland Europe %	North America %	Rest of world %
Holiday	53	50	52	69	50
Visiting friends or relatives	28	34	19	19	28
Business	12	12	14	8	13
Other	7	4	15	4	9

Where they stayed in the Republic of Ireland 2003

	Total %	Britain %	Mainland Europe %	North America %	Rest of world %
Hotels	12	19	7	17	6
Guesthouses/B&Bs	15	15	12	23	8
Rented .	26	13	34	24	33
Caravan and camping	1	1	21	0	1
Hostels	3	1	4	3	6
Friends and relatives	29	44	20	20	309
Other	14	7	21	13	16
Total	**47.6**	**18.5**	**16.4**	**8.9**	**3.9**

Seasonality of tourism in the Republic of Ireland 2003

	Total %	Britain %	Mainland Europe %	North America %	Rest of world %
Jan–Mar	17	19	15	16	15
April	9	98	9	6	5
May	10	9	10	11	9
June	10	9	10	12	13
July	12	11	15	13	10
August	13	13	15	12	14
September	9	9	9	11	11
October–December	21	22	18	19	24

Note: Overseas tourist visits to Ireland in 2003 increased by 4.4% to 6.2 million. Tourist numbers from Britain increased by 3% and Mainland European tourists grew by almost 8%. Tourists from North American were up by 6% on the previous year.

Channel Islands

Volume and tourist spending in the Channel Islands 2001

	Visitors (millions)	Nights (millions)	Spending (£ millions)
UK and overseas residents	895,510	3.2	249

Purpose of visit to the Channel Islands

Holidays in the Channel Islands

	UK and overseas residents visitors (millions)		UK Residents visitors
Holiday	2.5	**Nights**	**Millions**
Visiting friends or relatives	0.4	1–3	107,733
Business	0.08	4–6	76,952
Other	0.22	7+	200,075
All purposes	3.2	**Total holidays**	384,760

Seasonality of tourism in the Channel Islands

	All on holiday/stay No. of trips	%
Jan, Feb, Mar	31,250	7
Apr, May, Jun	168,154	36
Jul, Aug, Sept	213,649	46
Oct, Nov, Dec	55,738	11

The Isle of Man

Scheduled passenger traffic 2001

	Numbers
Period visitors staying in paid accommodation	95,948
Period visitors staying with friends or relatives	105,345
Isle of Man residents	329,388
Business people	76,311
Day trippers	9,459
Total	616,451

TIP
Be sure you read up on the country of origin when your guests are from overseas.

In summary, global trends indicate that people travelling in the future will take more **short break holidays** than ever before. This is due to several different factors, among them the trickle down effect of changes in the workplace and by choice. Visitors will be better educated and more affluent, with high expectations of customer service and value for money.

DOMESTIC MARKET

The number of domestic trips undertaken by the general public is projected to expand in the future. Again, due to changes in the workplace, people will take more short breaks than ever before.

Stress in the workplace is already starting to produce a knock-on effect in personal relationships and subsequently, people will take more time out with their loved ones if only to resolve any rifts that might be emerging.

Holiday patterns are starting to change. Where in the past, holidaymakers predominately took extended weekends they are now finding that someone in their family may be employed on a part-time basis during the weekend, so they will have to take some of their break during the week. In the future, many accommodation houses will start to notice more evenness throughout the week as people take breaks to fit in with a deregulated workplace.

SHORT BREAK HOLIDAYS

The short break market has become increasingly significant in recent years with current tourism trends throughout the world moving in favour of one to three-night breaks rather than fortnightly holidays. Here is what Scottish Tourism has to say:

> Research over recent years has shown a definite international trend towards taking shorter main holidays, and for holidaymakers to take several shorter breaks during the year. The traditional two-week summer holiday is becoming less important for many people. There are thought to be a number of social trends affecting the marketplace, including, for example:
>
> ◆ The time-squeeze phenomenon – many people feel they have shorter windows of time in which to take holidays.
>
> ◆ Household size is falling – people have more to spend and are less constrained by school holidays.
>
> ◆ An ageing population – with more time to take more breaks.
>
> These social trends have already changed the nature of tourism. It is generally accepted that Scotland will take some time to recover its former position as a main holiday destination. On the other hand, Scottish tourism does have the opportunity to capitalise on the growing tendency to take short breaks and to utilise spare capacity out of the peak season.
>
> Growing the short breaks market is a key component of the New Strategy for Scottish Tourism.

3

Who Is Your Customer?

This chapter is all about helping you to focus on who you believe will be your customer. Why do you need to work this out now? Before you decide where you buy, what you are going to buy, or what renovations you will need to convert your existing property, you must know if the market, or customer base, can support your endeavour.

GETTING YOUR FACTS STRAIGHT

How do you go about finding the size of your potential market? If you have not been involved in tourism before, then you will have a limited idea as to why people come into your area, or for that matter, what your geographical location has to offer.

The starting point is to source where reliable information can be gathered on key issues such as location, costs, staff requirements, time constraints and a whole host of operating details. At this stage, potential Bed & Breakfast operators need answers, that is, facts and details upon which they can build a comprehensive picture of their proposed operation, the possible market, the methods of operation, etc. They need to undertake research to give them a realistic understanding of their prospective business.

Your Bed & Breakfast will not appeal to everybody. You should be identifying the type of guests you want to attract, that is, your preferred **target market**.

What type of guests would you like to attract to your B&B? The choice is yours – you should at this early stage make this decision. Would you prefer to be servicing the top end of the market or the general holidaymaker? Would you feel more comfortable with corporate clients or with family groups or groups of friends? Your choice of target market will be a vital factor in influencing your decision about where to locate and how to design your premises. If, on the other hand, you decide to use your existing dwelling with modifications, then you must determine what type of guest your Bed & Breakfast will attract.

The following table contains ten categories of target guests to help you to identify your prime market group and also your preference towards two subsidiary groups, listed in order. Socio economic considerations should apply in all categories, as should preferred age brackets.

Target market options

Market segment	Prime market	Subsidiary market 1	Subsidiary market 2
Affluent guests			
Couples			
Singles			
Families			
Corporate			
Guests with a disability			
Budget market			
Groups			
Gay/lesbian			
Other: Guests with pets, etc.			

Having identified your preferred market groups (this can also indicate age and income), you can now decide whether you are looking at a purely commercial venture, or if you are you considering a lifestyle adjustment still using your existing dwelling. You have two clear options:

1. **A commercial venture** – is a stand-alone business where the income is your prime source of revenue.

2. **A lifestyle adjustment** – is when you decide to get into Bed & Breakfast as a means of generating a top-up or secondary income and as a *sea change* option. This may well become a source of prime income in the future.

Once your decision has been made as to what type of Bed & Breakfast business you want to run, we suggest you visit your local **tourist information centre** to get the most recent facts and figures on how many visitors your preferred area attracts per year. You will find out how old they are, what they do, how long they stay, what and why they are visiting. The centre may also be able to advise you how many other accommodation suppliers are in your area, their average occupancy rate, and any other information regarding the visitors to your area.

Contact your **regional tourism board**. They can give you up-to-date information on the type of holidays and accommodation people are choosing in your area. You should be able to ascertain the trends that are occurring. If you notice discrepancies when comparing the data collected, you might be able to bridge, or fill, any gaps. You can obtain the latest tourism trends, as it applies to your area, by using the contact addresses listed in Useful Addresses.

FAST FACTS

The following are some facts that will help to put the information you are seeking into some context. It could also be of some assistance with various sections of your **feasibility study** or **business plan**.

Research indicates that over the next five years, the domestic market will be taking short break holidays, usually 2 nights and 3 days, with more frequency than ever before. Many people surveyed said they would be undertaking this break with their partner, but without children. Thirty per cent said this break would be in their own country.

Many more women are travelling for both leisure and business as their roles in the workplace become more significant.

Progressively, more people will use the internet to book holidays and they will often be last minute bookings after destinations and prices have been compared. They will be seeking new experiences and a better understanding of the culture in the areas visited. More visitors are choosing their destinations based on their specific interests, for example, researching family history.

Tourism is predicted to grow substantially in the coming years, with the annual world-spending on all leisure and business travel expected to double to £3 trillion over the next 10 years.

There are a few other things you should be aware of. As we know, the world is constantly changing. Rapid and geographically unbalanced economic growth has been predicted to come to an end in the middle of this century. Over this period, the world is predicted to move from the present situation of income inequality, with low average wages, to reasonable income equality, with much higher average income.

Between now and 2050 the world's income is forecast to increase ten-fold. The largest economies will be in Asia. However, among the ten biggest economies, per capita income is expected to remain the highest in the USA.

The key demographic development is the death rate. If, as some people maintain, average life expectancy will move to about 100 years, the world's population may stabilise at approximately ten billion. However, if medical causes of death are lessened by medical progress, then world population may pass ten billion, and keep rising for some time, at about one billion per decade.

People are living longer. And there are far more of them. This means two things for you:

- retired people need something to supplement their income in their golden years – which in effect could be 30–40; and

- they will want somewhere to go on a short break holiday within a two to three hour driving distance from their home, Bed & Breakfasts being a favoured accommodation choice.

It is projected that by the year 2005, more than 31% of the UK and Irish work force could be employed on a part-time basis. This means that those of us, who for the future, want to earn the same income that we currently enjoy, will need to have two or three part-time jobs. These won't necessarily be in the same industry. People will have to up-skill in order to get these jobs. To be one of the 69% still employed full time you will need to be highly skilled and trained and be willing to further your education at every opportunity.

Rather than face this ultra-competitive job market, many older (and some younger) people are becoming consultants or contractors. Instead, however, of falling into the 1980's trap of renting an expensive office in a good suburb, they are working out of their high-tech office at home. B&Bs are a great way to help supplement the peaks and troughs of a consultancy business, if your property is in a suitable location.

We have found that 75% of people who are exploring the idea of entering the Bed & Breakfast market are corporate workers doing so as a financial contingency plan for their future. The other 25% do so for emotional reasons. Bed & Breakfasts are a soft financial risk. You may own your own home. If you don't get a lot of bookings you still own your home – you haven't lost your financial shirt.

What about retailing as a way to earn an income after 40? Recent studies found that 50% of all boutique retailers barely cover their rent and their employees' wages. The hours spent out of their home in their shop increases every year, as consumers want to shop when they are not working. Remember, we are all working longer and longer hours.

Which brings us to another point in the B&B's favour.

Traditionally people worked 9–5, Monday to Friday. If you owned a Bed & Breakfast that focused on the domestic market, then your business was restricted, primarily, to weekends. With the increase of flexible working hours and the decrease of the mid-year, two to three week holiday, more people are choosing several **short holiday breaks** throughout the year, often mid-week, or as an adjunct to their weekend.

TIP

Keep yourself up to date with the short-break holiday trends. This market segment is already gathering pace.

It is estimated that 70% of people had not taken all their accrued holidays in the past year. Of these, 40% had not taken any leave in the past year, with more than half not having had a holiday for more than two years. Job security concerns are being touted as the likely reason for this, the trend being that people are much more comfortable having a short break holiday, than leaving their office for extended periods. Employers and governments are being pressured into encouraging their employees to take leave.

CAPTURING YOUR TARGET MARKET

So how can you capture your target market? Make no mistake about it – to be a success at Bed & Breakfast you need to capture it. Bed & Breakfasts in cities are becoming a more and more attractive option. Being close to a business district is becoming a desirable location. There needs to be a reason for people to go to your area – something to do as well as to take a rest. Are you near a national park and walking tracks? Or are you close to a tourist area, for example, the Lake District, Snowdonia, Loch Ness, the Southern Irish Coast, the Giant's Causeway? Are you in a popular country town such as St Ives, Keswick, Inverness, Abergavenny, Banbridge or Waterford? Are you in a high-density commercial area? These are the factors you need to consider before you start.

If you want to attract a particular type of person, for example, executives visiting your city for conferences, make sure that they will feel at home with you and your partner or family. Ideally, your target market should be people like you, or who like the things you like – if it is, in the long run your business will be a greater success.

You also need to ensure that your proposed customers come into your area in reasonable numbers. Have you checked that they are coming to your area now?

If you want to attract **business** or **corporate clients** you will need to look at your local community and its market potential. Are companies attracted to your area for conferences? Is your local council doing a lot to attract businesses to relocate to your area? You need to ensure your council and tourist office understands the service you can provide, for example, being able to show these visitors the 'real' experience of your community.

Have you thought about academics? Does your town have a **university** or a **tertiary college**? Introduce yourself to the person responsible for booking the accommodation for their visitors, send them your promotional literature and invite them to come to stay for a night. If they enjoy their stay they are more likely to book with you.

If, like many B&Bs, you see your market to be **overseas guests**, you need to investigate why tourists are attracted to your area. Is it the local markets? Historic areas? The best beach on the coast of Cornwall, or the pubs? While determining this, by visiting your tourist centre to check their research on visitor numbers, you also need to find out the **age** of the people visiting your area. This information will help you to determine the facilities you need to provide to attract this market. It also helps you to spend your promotional budget wisely.

NICHE MARKETS

This brings us to **niche markets**. Within the tourist sector you may want to specialise in a particular type of tourist, usually a person who is attracted specifically to your area, or shares your interest or passion. Some examples of this are fishermen, hikers, birdwatchers, history buffs, and people wanting a romantic getaway.

To target a particular niche you may need to consider the following:

- *That you have particular knowledge of that market yourself.* If your area is known for its fauna and flora and you intend to exploit this market, you will need to know about this yourself. It would help if you had contact with a naturalist or a local ranger, who could give guided walks or hold weekend workshops for visitors.

- *You may need to supply special facilities.* If your passion is cooking and you are going to run a creative cooking school, you may need to change the layout of your kitchen in order to support this.

- *You might look at special décor.* If your niche is going to be trout fishermen you may want to consider attractive photos in your hallway of local fishing spots, or display a mounted trophy. A word of caution here. Don't go overboard, as you don't want to put other guests off. A few details here and there will provide a conversation point.

◆ *Promotion*. You need to launch your entry into the market with advertising and editorial in appropriate journals. Offer influential people and decision makers within your niche community a weekend away at your Bed & Breakfast. It is positive word of mouth that will assist in promoting your speciality.

There are major groups that people are targeting with great success. We will discuss them now in detail.

THE CORPORATE MARKET

Some B&B operators capture the **corporate market** mid-week and the leisure market during the weekends. If you have travelled extensively on business then you would agree that the part we all detested was dining by ourselves! Bed & Breakfasts can supply the corporate traveller with a degree of normality during their trip.

🏨 🏨 Some larger Bed & Breakfasts and Guesthouses are targeting corporate business to stage strategy meetings at their establishment. To do this successfully you need the right facilities, such as a meeting room, computers for PowerPoint demonstrations,

> **TIP**
>
> Estate agents and community organisations such as Rotary and Lions Clubs are a good source to access the corporate market.

slide projectors, whiteboards, markers, photocopiers, faxes, full catering facilities, etc. For larger establishments this can be quite lucrative. Your guests will probably want to check their email so an additional phone line would be useful.

SINGLE TRAVELLERS

There are, in many countries, many **single people** who only talk to people at work; they go home by themselves, to themselves. They need a holiday too, even if it is just to meet and talk to others.

Single travellers often want to know the real heart of a city or town and meeting the locals is part of that. What better way to meet the locals than to stay in their home? You need to be centrally located and close to transport. You will not win any points if your guest needs to travel in poorly lit, suburban streets to reach the local bus stop or train station.

■ Please do single travellers a favour and don't banish them to your smallest, dingiest room. Remember that the single traveller is paying more per head than the average couple, and they are eating less, using less electricity and hot water. Treat them well and they will return the favour, recommending you to other single travellers.

WOMEN TRAVELLERS

The **single female traveller** is an ever-growing market – both as part of work and as part of adventure. Some women, however, feel uncomfortable sitting by themselves having dinner. If they go to a restaurant alone they are in danger of attracting unwanted attention from the opposite sex, or they feel trapped in their room if they order room service. Bed & Breakfasts are a great alternative to this, particularly those that offer the option of an evening meal.

■ For the single woman the Bed & Breakfast offers conversation without pressure as well as a homely touch. Some Bed & Breakfasts are targeting the corporate end of this market quite successfully, appealing to the safety angle and the gregarious nature of women. Remember if you are going to try for this market it can be difficult to access from the suburbs. An inner city location, close to good restaurants, attractions and transport, would be a viable option.

ALTERNATIVE LIFESTYLES

The so-called **pink dollar** is often talked about as a lucrative market and, of course, some Bed & Breakfasts are run by gay couples. Your customers are often well paid with a high disposable income. Word of mouth works very well here. You could alert potential visitors by advertising in the gay press. The Internet is also another powerful tool for this market. Your customers are usually computer literate and will use their computers to book their short breaks. This market is not for everyone, but if you're comfortable with it, and it must be said that if you are going to run a Bed & Breakfast you will need to be open minded, you will attract a loyal customer base.

PEOPLE WITH A DISABILITY

This group, like any other, both likes to travel for pleasure and needs to travel with work. Remember that only a small percentage of people who come under this heading use a wheelchair. They do, however, often have **special needs**. If you are purpose-building a Bed & Breakfast you might like to consider this group. There are some statutory requirements to adhere to, so it is suggested that you obtain a copy of the appropriate Act from the Stationery Office or download it free of charge at: www.disability.gov.uk

Again this is a very loyal group, with great word of mouth potential. If you can cater for their special needs they will frequent your B&B. You will find that many of the modifications you will make for the disabled also apply for the elderly.

DIETARY REQUIREMENTS

Some Bed & Breakfasts have had success with guests with particular **dietary requirements**: vegan, gluten-free, vegetarian and kosher. We would suggest you only try to cater for these groups if you share their predilections, as they want meals that are tasty. Usually, only someone who understands their needs has the ability to cater successfully for these groups.

THE FAMILY MARKET

There is a growing need for some Bed & Breakfasts to cater specifically for the **family market** with the development of well designed suites that can serve the multi-purpose requirements of family and group accommodation, and can also revert to separate accommodation. The biggest opportunities are for those who are located in an area where there is a lot for children to do: swim, fish, ride horses, walk, visit historic sites and be close to a major attraction, etc.

Self-contained cottages, where the host provides a breakfast, often in the form of a basket meal, is becoming a very popular choice for families. At the moment most Bed & Breakfasts are giving this market to caravan parks, which are refurbishing and building cabins at a rapid rate. B&B operators who cater for this market should do well, given that it is generally accepted as being affordable.

You will need to contact your relevant local authority before considering self-catering accommodation.

Another popular place to cater for families is a Bed & Breakfast on a **farm**. If you go down this road you need to create almost a storybook farm on your property, with sheep, cats, dogs, pigs and chickens children can feed, ponies they can ride, and a cow or a goat the children can hand milk. All this with appropriate adult supervision, of course! For the city child this would represent the adventure of a lifetime. Please be sure to talk to your insurance provider if you plan to offer activities such as these.

Some authorities will require specific zoning before you will be allowed to go ahead and again, it is suggested that you obtain a copy of your relevant local government and housing requirements to see whether your property is suitably classified.

DO'S AND DON'TS

In this age of litigation we wanted to explore how the Bed & Breakfast operator is affected by advertising 'No smoking', 'No children', and 'No pets'. Various government departments were contacted to try to ascertain how the Bed & Breakfast operator was placed in relation to these exclusions and to anti-discrimination laws.

It was found that in this area, government departments tend to be reactive, rather than proactive. In other words, they will wait until a member of the public makes a complaint about any restriction before making a judgement.

There are many strategies you can adopt in order to handle difficult situations should they arise.

NO PETS

There are hygiene and health, not to mention safety reasons, why you should not allow **pets** in your B&B unless you have suitable accommodation for them. If you have your own pets you will need to advertise this to potential guests. There may be valid reasons why guests prefer to stay where there are no pets. For example, they may be allergic to them. Have handy the name of a local kennel that houses cats and dogs so that you can recommend them to potential guests.

Some B&Bs, however, are successfully targeting this market and acting as hosts to animals. You would need to clearly map out your intentions to your local authority to ensure that you have all areas covered before you advertise the fact. You should also advise your insurers that you are catering for animals as it may have an effect on your annual premium.

NO SMOKING

We believe that this is a valid 'don't'. Smoke gets into fabrics and furnishings and is impossible to remove completely before new guests arrive. However, we would suggest that you provide a sheltered area outside where your guests can smoke. Provide an ashtray (which you clean at least twice daily) and a small rubbish bin. This will prevent butts littering your garden. When advising potential guests of your property inform them of your policy, but let them know about the smoking area outside.

NO CHILDREN

This is the tricky one. An anti-discrimination act (see below), prohibits discrimination on account of age. Saying, 'No children allowed' or 'Children not welcome' could be seen as discrimination against an age group.

This can be a dilemma however, as you will find that some guests who want to experience selected types of accommodation do so to have a break together. You may choose only to cater for families with children at certain times, for example school holidays.

If you don't wish children to stay it is better to say: 'We don't have the facilities to cater for children'. If you do want to welcome children this could be developed as an interesting and lucrative niche market. But remember children will behave like children and you need to be prepared for what that may mean.

We also suggest that you obtain a free copy of the 'Children Act' titled, 'A guide to help you with day registration' or download it at: www.doh.gov.uk/busguid/childact.htm

ANTI-DISCRIMINATION LAWS AND THE B&B HOST

Over the last few years there has been an increase in discussion about the rights of smokers, children and the disabled. In a society that is becoming more litigious, B&B operators need to know their position in respect of new developments in anti-discrimination. Do Bed & Breakfast operators have special rights in light of the fact that they live on the premises and their business is also their home? In researching this we came up with the following items of interest:

Question: Is there a law that would prohibit B&B operators from having a 'no children as guests' policy? For example, they may not have adequate facilities to cater for young children.

Answer: All government areas have what they call 'Parental Status and an Ageing Policy' which states quite clearly that no one in business can discriminate on age. If your B&B preference were not to have minors as guests, then to say that you don't have facilities for children would not be enough to stop a prospective guest from lodging a discrimination complaint against you. You can, however, apply for an exemption to this ruling. Your argument would need to be very well thought through and soundly based to have any chance of succeeding. Consider saying, 'Our property is not suitable for children as there are no facilities to keep them entertained'. In this way you have warned the reader in your advertisement that the children might not have enough to keep them occupied. Most parents reading comments like that would select another property.

Question: Does the law require a B&B operator to provide wheelchair access?

Answer: Wheelchair access is not mandatory as some dwellings are not suitable for this type of access by their very nature, but again, there are no grounds to discriminate against someone who uses a wheelchair and wishes to stay at your B&B. It is implicit in this situation, that means of accessing the facilities are within the reach of your guest.

Question: Can a B&B operator enforce a 'no smoking' policy?

Answer: You can specify no smoking on your property by placing 'Thank you for not smoking' signs in appropriate areas. There does not appear to be a law that states you can't specify no smoking although this, as with many areas of anti-discrimination laws, needs to be tested in the courts.

Question: Is it reasonable for a B&B operator to take the following view: 'Because my B&B is the place where I live, I can set policy and make rules that would not be possible if the property was a large hotel or guesthouse?'

Answer: Not really, if it means that discrimination factors are ignored and the law is broken. Common sense should prevail when dealing with these issues because litigation is both lengthy and costly. By couching your words carefully when advertising features pertaining to your B&B, readers will be able to decide whether your Bed & Breakfast property is suitable for their situation. In considering this point, remember that people do not appreciate being misled. It is important that you keep abreast of anti-discrimination policy and subscribe to publications that can enlighten you on the issues that concern you and your Bed & Breakfast.

TIP

As you collect information on your area, brochures, books and the like, keep them for later use.

4

Preparing Your Property

The first decision you need to make when entering the short break holiday market is whether you are going to be a 'traditional' Bed & Breakfast with a few rooms and a cosy atmosphere, or will you opt for a guesthouse or a small hotel, where there is more separation between you and your guests? The difference is governed by statutory requirements in some places and only you can make the decision as to how you wish to operate.

The main reason people choose the traditional Bed & Breakfast option is because the house they currently own has sufficent space to accommodate both themselves and potential guests. There are benefits: your guests have easy access to you, it is easier to keep an eye on your property and you do not have to commute to work. The negatives are that having a family life can be constrained by your guests, that you need to be conscious that guests can access your personal space, and it is hard to escape from work.

What is the best option? The main thing you need to consider is **privacy**. No matter which route you choose – or due to property or financial constraints, have chosen for you – you need to ensure you and your family have some personal space where guests are unable to intrude. This is a statutory requirement throughout Ireland.

Your family area should include a bathroom, bedrooms and preferably a separate lounge or family room. Without this space the strain on your personal relationships may be too much to bear. It is also good for your guests, as they are less likely to feel they are intruding on someone else's life. This space is particularly important if you have children or grandchildren living with you.

LOCATION

Position, position! For many reasons this could be the single most important part of establishing a successful Bed & Breakfast.

The location of your Bed & Breakfast in relation to your market really could make the difference as to whether your enterprise will succeed or fail. An important factor to remember is that guests often like to be within walking distance of food and drink establishments.

In order to determine whether your property is in the right position, remember to consider both people on touring holidays as well as those who are having a short break holiday, the latter often within a short driving time from their home. International guests may want to look for properties that are close to public transport facilities.

To be a roaring success, with good occupancy, you need to appeal to both markets. Ask yourself the following questions about your property or the one you are thinking of purchasing:

◆ Is my property near a main road or in a country town with easy access?

◆ Is my property a farm or 'country house' (i.e. definitely in a rural setting)?

◆ Is my property in a tourist area? Factor into your profit and loss projections the seasonality of the area and the likelihood your bookings may fluctuate.

◆ Is my property within a large metropolitan city? Be sure your property is aimed at an appropriate market if it is in a suburban area and that it is well sign-posted (always consult your local authority before erecting any directional signs), as your guests will not want to spend all their time finding you. It can be an advantage to be close to public transport, especially for those guests who are touring, and also to be close to popular attractions. If you are targeting the corporate market your guests will need good access to, and to be within easy travelling distance of the business district.

LOCAL GOVERNMENT AND YOUR BED & BREAKFAST

Before you march headlong into deciding where you are going to set up your Bed & Breakfast, or whether you are going to convert your current home, you need to establish a relationship with your local authority.

There is a raft of **planning permission** and **building regulations** that can apply to those offering serviced or self-catering accommodation. As an example, if you are considering structural changes to an existing dwelling or adding an extension, it is vital that you contact your local authority for their advice and/or permission.

Policies on granting planning permission do vary, for example, on car parking facilities and the number of guest rooms. Even if you feel that your home has the facilities set down by local authorities, a **change of use planning permission** may still be required. Another suggestion is to get a copy of the relevant authority's planning approval guide.

For those of you who are planning something a little more ambitious you might want to hire a consultant to act on your behalf. At their worst, relevant authorities can require mountains of documentation and it can save a lot of headaches if you hire a professional.

If you want to make a complaint against the handling of your application, you should first contact the authority itself. If you are still dissatisfied, lodge a complaint with a higher authority. When there is conflict it is best to be guided by your own legal adviser or a private planning consultant.

TO CONVERT, BUY OR BUILD?

You need to establish whether you are going to **convert** the home you already live in, **buy** a new property, or **custom build** a property if you can find suitable land. Each option has its merits – what you choose will depend on your personal circumstance. If you only want your Bed & Breakfast to give you pocket money, a supplement to an already healthy financial position, we would suggest you convert the property you already have. If you want your B&B to provide you with a little more financially, and if your house is not in a major city or a tourist area you may need to consider either buying an existing property or custom-building one.

> **TIP**
>
> Consider self-contained cottages if you have young children as you will maintain greater privacy and reduce the chance of burnout.

AN EXERCISE IN FINANCIAL VIABILITY

To test the viability of getting your house ready for a Bed & Breakfast the following can be used as a benchmark. Using your notebook go into all the areas of your property that guests will encounter, taking notes about what needs doing in each of these spaces. Be sure to look at these areas through *the eyes of a paying guest* or ask someone else to do it for you. If you do this exercise through the eyes of the resident property owner you will be in danger of deluding yourself. You are going into Bed & Breakfast to succeed. Therefore you need to view the property as a potential guest and so charge as much as needed, without being excessive. In this way the maximum occupancy that you can comfortably handle can be realised. You will not achieve these goals if your product is not right.

You need to look at the following in every room:

Ceiling
◆ Is the ceiling flaking?

◆ Are there any damp patches?

◆ Does it need repainting?

Walls
◆ Is the paintwork in good condition and painted a colour that adds to the ambience of a guest bedroom and the look of your B&B?

◆ Are there cracks or any structural problems?

◆ Do you need to strip wallpaper or replace it?

Flooring
◆ Is the carpet or flooring in good condition or does it need shampooing or polishing?

◆ If the floor is polished timber then do you need to revarnish or stain?

General

◆ How soundproof is your house? This is particularly important in bedrooms, as nothing is more off-putting, or uncomfortable, than being aware of other people's more intimate moments.

◆ Is there adequate ventilation?

◆ Is there adequate lighting?

◆ Are there any structural problems?

◆ Is there enough space to give every guest bedroom an en suite or bathroom? If your room rate is going to be high, your guests' expectation would be their very own fully-equipped guest bathroom, possibly even with a spa bath.

◆ Is there enough storage area or wardrobe space in each guest bedroom?

◆ Is appropriate fire safety installed? In most instances a regular, legal inspection is required.

◆ Is there an adequate supply of hot water?

Later in this chapter we discuss all the extras you will need to consider when converting your house into a Bed & Breakfast.

Once you have decided what work you need to do, ascertain what work you can do yourself and where you will need a professional.

Obviously, the more you can do yourself the better off financially you will be. The things you need professionals for should be listed.

You then need to get at least three quotes for everything. It is worth the time and the effort.

After you have done all these things, you need to compare the cost with a projection of what you think you can earn. How much is too much money? As a general rule, you should only spend what you think you can get back when selling your property as a house, not as a Bed & Breakfast.

TIPS FOR BUYING AN ESTABLISHED B&B

You have done the research and realised that your home just won't adequately convert to a Bed & Breakfast. Plus you have decided that you want to make this your sole livelihood. You have a bit of money in the bank and you believe the best thing to do is buy an **established** Bed & Breakfast. That way you should have a good income from day one.

When looking to purchase an established Bed & Breakfast you need to consider why the business is for sale:

- Is the area the Bed & Breakfast is in overpopulated with accommodation providers and therefore bookings are low?

- Are the owners experiencing B&B burnout? (It happens!)

- Do they have children who have reached teenage years and the lifestyle is just too difficult to juggle?

- Is there a motorway or other development to be built which will affect the area?

The first and last reasons are what you need to consider. The middle ones could mean you might have a viable property.

- How old is the business and how many of the years have been profitable? Have they been making a profit for the last couple of years?

- How much business is currently booked for the next 6 months? Ask to see the reservations diary.

- Ask to see the visitors' book. Guests don't lie. If the business is well loved you should see it from the book. It also helps you understand what the guests love about the place. Is the success tied up in the current owners? The cooking? The nearby historical sights? The architecture of the house?

- What percentage of the Bed & Breakfast's business is made up of return customers? How much, therefore, are you paying for 'goodwill', that is, the intangible contribution of the current owners? Is it valid?

- Do the books look accurate? Do the assets outweigh the liabilities? Get the opinion of your solicitor, bank manager, accountant or financial adviser.

- Have all renovations been undertaken with the necessary approval? Is the property zoned for Bed & Breakfast operation?

- As with the purchase of any property, location is an important thing to consider. You cannot be in an area where the reasons to stay are too limited for the business to be viable. Does the B&B have the right qualities?

- Is the current operator irretrievably connected to the success of the Bed & Breakfast? Are they award-winning chefs who bring food connoisseurs to the establishment? Will your relative lack of culinary expertise be the downfall of the Bed & Breakfast?

CONVERT TO WHAT?

If you are to turn your current house into a B&B you will, undoubtedly, need to make some changes. Guests choose B&Bs for their homely atmosphere, but what they want is the picture book version of home – not the reality.

They don't want the family fights, the untidiness, the washing, the laundry, the cooking or cleaning, or the discussions on what to watch on TV. They want the conveniences of a hotel, but with a home-cooked meal, pleasant discussion, and touches such as fresh flowers and home-made biscuits. They want a room filled with good books, a bathroom with complimentary bath salts and oils, and the smell of freshly baked scones and freshly ground coffee. And increasingly they want an en suite or bathroom of their own.

When assessing the changes you will need to make to your property to cater for guests you will need to start from the outside in.

SIGNAGE

The cheapest way you can get your B&B noticed is with a **sign**. It needs to be in the style of your B&B's architecture, your other promotional material (stationery, etc) and your area. Use a professional signwriter – the sign will create a first impression, and it needs to denote professionalism.

Before contracting a signwriter or graphic designer to work on your behalf you will need to contact your local authority. There are invariably regulations on signage placement, height and type and sometimes on colours, particularly if it's illuminated. It's cheaper to find out the restrictions before you are the proud owner of a sign you are unable to display.

It's also a good idea to ensure the name and street number of your establishment is clear to read day or night.

TIP

You never get a second chance to make a first impression. First impressions last.

Nothing puts guests in a bad mood more than being unable to find your establishment if your street name or house number is hidden behind a hedge or cannot be read on a dark, wet night.

FIRST IMPRESSIONS COUNT

The first sight your guests have of your B&B will be the **impression** they will take with them. It won't matter what they find on the inside of your establishment, that first look of your unkempt gardens and a dilapidated fence will stay with them throughout their whole stay. That is, if they bother to come in at all.

The truth is, first impressions count. What you can get away with in your own home you cannot get away with as a proprietor of a Bed & Breakfast. The outside appearance of your establishment helps to set the tone of your business. Use the following checklist to help ensure that the first impression is a good one.

- The lawn is mown regularly.

- The path to the front door is free from overgrown bushes and hedges.

- The path is free from cracks and weeds.

- If the house is made of bricks then be sure they are clean.

- Repaint when necessary. When you do repaint, don't paint over a problem. It will recur. Cure the problem first, then paint.

◆ The fence is in good condition.

◆ The entrance is free from spider webs.

◆ Letterboxes, door handles and windows are clean and polished.

◆ Light bulbs are changed as soon as needed.

◆ The outside is well lit at night.

◆ The garden is regularly tended, with no dead plants.

◆ Any steps or tiling are swept and cleaned regularly – and checked for slipperiness.

◆ 🏠 🏠 Signage to car parking and reception is clearly visible.

As for your **garden**, you need it to be as attractive as you can make it. When planning your garden think about the time you can realistically afford to spend maintaining it and design it accordingly.

In the summer months, it is a good idea to have some garden furniture so your guests can enjoy the sunshine and have some outdoor privacy. The advantage of this is that it's also a great place for you and your family to enjoy the sunshine and some privacy.

Think about the addition of a water feature of some sort. Not only are they aesthetically pleasing, but the sound is very soothing – just what you need in a Bed & Breakfast. Not to mention the fact that it is very good feng shui. The Chinese believe that water is the symbol of money. A water feature will help attract more money into your home. (They say!)

THE ENTRANCE

The **entrance** is the first thing your guests will see on arrival at your establishment. It is your chance to impress them from the word go. You want touches that will exude warmth and friendliness. Go for a huge bunch of fresh flowers, a feature wall in a bright colour or an original piece of artwork. If your hall is narrow it might be a good idea to add a large mirror to help convey a sense of spaciousness.

It is a good idea not to go overboard with furniture in an entrance as it can create an obstacle course when carrying luggage. An umbrella stand and a coat rack or cupboard are ideal additions. You don't want guests traipsing water throughout the house. They will be pleased with your thoughtfulness.

Flooring deserves special consideration in your porch and hallway. You want a surface that is easy to keep clean and is hard wearing. Tiles need to be non-slip, or if you have floorboards you must ensure any polish is not slippery. If you choose carpet you should investigate commercial carpet – it is more durable and easier to keep clean than domestic grade carpets.

Heating or cooling is another consideration. If you are surrounded by snow you want your entry to feel like a warm cocoon. Likewise, if it happens to be hot and humid you want your guests' first impression to be one of coolness and freshness.

LIVING ROOMS

As we stated in the last chapter, it is important, if at all possible, for both you and your guests' sanity to have some separate space, other than your respective bedrooms. We would suggest that the best option would be a **lounge** room, or similar type of room. For some properties, it might be your old family room, conservatory or former children's playroom. This room will give your guests space and allow them to feel more at home. The fact that you will have a separate lounge gives you a place to escape that feels all yours, not the property of the general public.

Research indicates that guests don't mind sharing living room areas with each other, providing they can identify where they can sit. For example, if you have a living area available for two guest bedrooms then rearrange your furniture so that you have two settings. You don't want people trapped in their bedroom. Guests generally don't mind if other guests share their space, or even if it is possible to overhear their conversation.

You need **entertainment facilities**, particularly music. An assortment of books is a great idea, covering all genres.

Board games are essential – people love to challenge their friends to a game. **Television** is another thing you will need to consider. Many people go to Bed & Breakfasts to escape from television, but others find it relaxing. One suggestion would be that if you are going to have televisions place them in the guest bedrooms (preferably in a cupboard) where they can make the choice to use them, or have a separate TV room. If, because of space limitations, you have to put a TV in the lounge, don't arrange all your seating to face it and, preferably, hide it in a cupboard.

Be sure to contact the TV Licensing Authority, as extra TVs may not be covered by your home licence.

One of our concerns is that of 'amenity creep'. Some B&Bs are emulating the atmosphere found in hotels from the lower end of the market. Don't do this, because people who choose to stay in Bed & Breakfasts do so for the homely comforts and to avoid the impersonal atmosphere of a hotel. For example, avoid a TV in a guest bedroom that swivels out from the wall.

People love to sit around an **open fire**, so if you have one, be sure to light it, particularly on dull or cold days. This would be a memorable feature of your lounge room and will be a source of good publicity for you. If you have it, flaunt it!

Likewise, if you have a view of the ocean or mountains, exploit it. These things are what guests go away for – the romantic ideal of home.

DINING ROOMS

As the name suggests, a vitally important part of a B&B is one meal – breakfast. This meal needs to be taken in a place that characterises the ambience of your establishment. As much care should be taken with the dining room as with the bedrooms.

In the United Kingdom and Ireland, B&Bs have taken many different approaches to dining. Many places follow the European tradition of one large table around which all guests sit. This works very well for dinner, if you are planning to offer this as an option. People will occasionally bring their own wine and, over a few glasses, feel happy talking with strangers.

One large, communal table, however, can present some problems at breakfast. Some people are a little shy in the mornings and tend to keep to themselves. A number of establishments have found that they needed to introduce a breakfast area made up of a few tables of two and/or four settings, or a large and a small table.

It is a statutory requirement in some areas to have a separate breakfast table for each guest bedroom.

As for style, you need to create a room that both looks good and is practical. Remember you will be serving breakfast, so you want to be able to access all the seats. The table(s) can become a feature in the dining room, with an interesting centrepiece. Chairs should be comfortable. People on holidays won't want to rush eating so you want them to feel comfortable sitting for as long as they desire.

When buying **furniture** be aware of the upkeep. If your table is wood it will require work – you will need to protect it from moisture and heat.

You can get some great buys at places such as **second hand shops**. You also have the option of buying from a manufacturer or supplier of commercial catering furniture. For chairs, particularly, this may provide the best option for a larger establishment, as they will be comfortable, practical and hardwearing.

Ensure your dining room has a **sideboard** or bench of some kind. It makes it much easier when clearing tables and serving meals. It also has the added advantage of holding your dinner sets and cutlery. The only word of caution would be not to clutter the top with too many decorative items – keep it simple. If you have too much on it you will find difficulty in actually using it.

The **crockery** you use can demonstrate to your guests the style of your B&B. Remember it is the small things that your guests will describe to their friends.

Your everyday dinner set, with its scratches, chips and cracks will not do for paying guests. That doesn't mean you should buy Wedgwood or Royal Doulton, although for some of you that might be appropriate.

We would suggest crockery should be commercial quality. Any patterns should be under a thick glaze and able to withstand dishwashers at high temperatures. Tapered edges are more prone to chipping, so if you or your partner are clumsy, we would suggest choosing crockery with a rolled edge. Enquire in a retail outlet if there is a piece of china that could be tested for durability. Ask if the retailer has a discarded piece of the china of the type you are interested in purchasing, in order to test the glazing, or enquire about guarantees for the durability of the surface. The glazing can be assessed by running a knife across a glazed surface and seeing if it marks. If you see a flaw keep looking. Do not scrimp on china by buying the cheapest and, whatever you do, don't buy end of line china. Pieces will chip and break and you need a set for which you can easily purchase replacements or additions as required.

Remember you want china that is ovenproof, particularly if you are planning to offer dinner, and any china with a metal embossing, such as a gold rim, may not be suitable to be put in a microwave.

🏠 🏠 Commercial sets might be a good option for the larger Bed & Breakfasts and Guesthouses as your crockery may take quite a beating. This doesn't mean you still can't demonstrate personal style. Buy some beautiful serving plates and dishes. Use beautiful cutlery and glasses. Use the best napkins you can afford.

Choose a style of china, glassware and linen that reflect the style of your home, and which may be a feature of your region.

Your **glasses** should complement your china. In some cases, where a B&B does not have an alcohol licence, guests may be able to bring alcohol, with your permission, whether you provide an evening meal or not. At the very least you will need glasses for red and white wine, sherry, port, champagne, mixed drinks, and water, soft drinks or cordial.

Cutlery needs special consideration for your Bed & Breakfast. Stainless steel is easier to look after than silver, not least because you will be able to put it in the dishwasher. It will still stain and smear, however. To minimise this a good tip is to use boiling hot water and vinegar and wipe it with a linen tea towel once a week after it has been cleaned in a dishwasher.

Ornate designs can look wonderful, but are more difficult to keep clean. Choose cutlery made in one piece as grease and bacteria have a tendency to get caught between the blade and the handle. Plastic, bone and wooden handles are not always a good idea, as they will not withstand the dishwasher. As you can see, you need to balance style considerations with practical ones. Do you want to be cleaning that beautiful silver cutlery every day? Remember that you do want the table to look special when set, so choose wisely.

THE KITCHEN

While design and size of the **kitchen** will vary tremendously in Bed & Breakfasts this is still a main cog in the machine. Your kitchen may be used for cooking only or may have an eat-in function, which, while unsuitable or unlawful for guests, will be great for your family's privacy.

The main thing you need to ensure is **cleanliness**. You are now serving food to the general public and you need to treat this with the seriousness it deserves. The last thing you want is to risk food poisoning. You will need to contact your local authority to see what restrictions will affect you in your kitchen, eg, larger B&Bs must have a separate refrigerator for the guests' food. Increasingly, there is a legal requirement for those preparing food for the general public to obtain a recognised qualification. This will cover all aspects of food handling, storage and preparation. Your local Environmental Health Officer will have all the details.

The larger your establishment, the more likely you will be affected by commercial laws of one kind or another.

Make sure that all of your electrical equipment is safe as you have the responsibility to comply with the regulations set down. See your local authority about regulations and inspection requirements.

For health reasons, cutting boards should be labelled. For example, green for vegetables, red for meat, with matching colour-coded wiping cloths. Once again, it's a good idea to obtain a copy of the relevant health and safety legislation to be sure that your equipment complies with the relevant standards.

When it comes to design you need to remember preparing meals for a number of guests will require significant workspace in the form of a large bench and/or table.

At the minimum you will want a dishwasher, a microwave and an extractor fan. You might also need to consider a bigger fridge, and a pantry.

The other thing you must consider is safety. Kitchens need to be safe places in which to work. Kitchens and bathrooms are the most dangerous places in a home. Flooring needs special attention, for example, any tiles need to be the non-slip variety.

When it comes to kitchens, local government requirements tend to vary depending on the number of guest rooms applied for by the property owner. The best advice is to contact your local authority before making any drastic changes to your kitchen. Research has discovered that there may be changes regarding requirements for kitchens in the near future.

The average residential B&B would require a double sink and dishwasher. High quality detergent must be used due to the fact that the average domestic dishwasher does not heat to 60° Celsius.

B&Bs who offer an evening meal would require all the above but the dishwasher might need to be semi-industrial.

B&Bs that have an attached dining room with a restaurant will need to comply with standard restaurant regulations.

BATHROOMS AND TOILETS

The days of expecting your guests to share the family **bathroom** are basically gone. That is not to say you can't run a B&B if you don't have separate bathrooms or en suites for each guestroom. It means that you may not be able to have a room rate that is viable or an occupancy rate that is acceptable.

If you do elect to run with the family bathroom proposition then be sure you have sufficient cabinets that hide the family's gear. If it's a grand and elegant B&B you have in mind, and the room rate reflects this, then the guest's expectation will be to access a fully equipped bathroom. This may include a spa-bath.

To en suite or not to en suite that is the question. If you can only afford to do one major thing to convert your family home into a Bed & Breakfast, installing en suites is what you should spend your money on. More bookings are lost for not having en suites than for any other reason, especially with international travellers. Guests will happily pay more for this option.

If you intend to accommodate people with disabilities then the bathroom and toilet facilities will need special consideration. You will need to consider safety rails, a hand held showerhead and widened doorways. Again, floor tiles need to be non-slip; the relevant authorities will supply you with all the necessary details.

Given that you have heating in your bathroom, you will also need an extractor fan to eradicate all the condensation that occurs.

Opening a window is not sufficient to maintain the controlled ventilation required to keep condensation, and in the long term, mould, at bay in bathrooms. If you have sufficient room between your bathroom ceiling and the roof, the most efficient way to cover heating, ventilation and lighting is by installing a three-in-one heater, fan and light. For a little extra expenditure you will have a bathroom that is well lit, warm and well ventilated.

We would suggest that you replace shower curtains with doors, as there is less chance for errant water, and thus accidents. Likewise, as another safety precaution, we would suggest that showers are not over your bath. This is another safety nightmare. If you must use shower curtains ensure that you wash them regularly. Nothing puts a guest off more than mould. Also ensure they are weighted at the bottom, so as not to wrap around your guests' legs when they are having a shower.

It is important to have efficient, easy to operate showers. Taps with a simple single action are the best ones. The flow of water from the showerhead also needs to be adequate. It is very hard to rinse long hair with a trickle of water!

You need to ensure you have a copious supply of hot water. This is not an area where one can economise. Guests will always remember the B&B where they had a cold shower, bath or shave, and it will not be looked on favourably when telling their friends of their holiday break.

All your doors should be fitted with locks, and windows should be made of opaque glass or fitted with blinds. Your guests want to feel as if their stay is a retreat and not a peep show. The locks are particularly important if guests are sharing a bathroom.

You also may need to consider adding power points to large bathrooms. Special waterproof points are available and are a legal requirement.

At the very least you need sufficient power points for two appliances, a shaver and a hairdryer.

Ideally the bathroom area should be self-contained, with the hand basin in the bathroom. This gives a classier atmosphere to the room. A separate toilet with a wash hand basin is also a valuable facility if you have the room.

When it comes to furniture in your bathroom, it should be kept to a minimum. However, you might like to consider a chair or stool. Ensure it won't be affected adversely by the dampness.

With bathrooms and en suites it is the extras that will win you brownie points with your guests. We suggest that you consider providing the following:

◆ Two good quality, generously sized, towels per person, which you change daily. You also need to provide a hand towel and two face cloths.

◆ Mini soaps, preferably from a place like a body shop or another aromatherapy retailer. You might even be lucky enough to find a local person who makes natural products. These will need to be changed after each guest. The provision of a soap dispenser is a good alternative.

◆ Make-up remover pads. This is a great idea, as it will prevent your guests using your towels for this purpose.

◆ Plenty of thick, luxurious-feeling, toilet paper. OK, so it's a hidden luxury. So many Bed & Breakfasts get this wrong. Don't scrimp and buy the cheap brand. Your guests will notice and will not be impressed. Ensure your spare rolls are in an easy to find place.

◆ Candles, and some matches. These are particularly recommended if you have a spa. Nothing is more relaxing or romantic than candlelight, and isn't romance one of the main reasons your guests have chosen the Bed & Breakfast experience?

◆ Fresh flowers, preferably from your garden, or a small plant, will brighten up the room and reinforce the impression that you are the nurturing type. Be aware that some guests may be allergic to fresh flowers, so you may want to advise them beforehand or be prepared to remove them.

◆ A hair dryer. Forgetful guests will love you for this.

◆ A waste bin with a lid. The more bins you provide the less mess you will need to tidy up later.

◆ Complimentary bath oils, shower caps, shampoos and conditioners. These are a real treat and everyone loves them.

THE BEDROOMS

If you are going after the luxury romantic getaway market you might consider having spa baths for each guest **bedroom**. At the high end of the market, they are a definite draw. You can, of course, get a higher room rate for the privilege.

Now to the 'bed' part of your B&B, the place where your guests will spend at least one third of their stay with you.

The first points of call are the beds. This is the most important investment in furniture you will make – and you really must consider buying new ones. It is your guests' opinion of the quality of your bed you will most be recommended for.

One of the most commonly asked questions is what should you look for when purchasing a bed. Firstly – buy wholesale.

As soon as you register your business you will gain allowances with a wide range of wholesalers, from bed linen and bed manufacturers, to hospitality suppliers. Take advantage of these and shop around.

It is suggested you buy contract quality. These beds have the added advantage of being built for multiple and varied sleepers – so they will last longer in the long run. Most importantly they are reinforced around the sides – the first place your guests will sit when entering their guestroom.

If you have a number of guest rooms, purchase queen beds, doubles are too small for most couples, and have at least one room with two single beds that will zip up into a queen or king size bed. With more and more friends travelling together, along with mothers and daughters and colleagues, the ability to offer twin beds will give your potential guests another reason to stay with you.

As for brands, we recommend Sealy. Why? They understand the needs of the hospitality industry, including B&Bs. The coverings all meet the UK furniture industry's stringent regulations. The single zip up model has the option of an all-over covering. All their commercial beds are Healthshield protected, which protects against the build up of mould, mildew, bacteria and dust mites. The coverings are fire retardant. Sealy also provide a service that will show you how to care for the bed longer term. Their contract division, which will deal directly with you, can provide you with substantial savings. See page 250 for Sealy's contact details.

A rack or suitable place for luggage in the guest bedroom is important. This prevents suitcases ending up on the bed, bringing with them dust or dirt from outside.

TIP

Leave extra pillows and towels in each guest bedroom.

You will need to supply electric blankets during the colder months. You need two pillows per person. You need at least two sets of bed linen per bed – more if you don't want to wash every day.

Think seriously about domestic linen if you are running a larger Bed & Breakfast. It won't be able to withstand the daily washes and will fade very quickly. Normal household bed sheets have an average life expectancy of 300 washes as against those used in the hospitality industry that are able to last for 500 washes – they are usually 50% polyester and 50% cotton. There are a number of linen suppliers to the hospitality industry and are listed in the telephone directory. Ensure that you have spares of everything (blankets, pillows, sheets) in a cupboard in the guestroom in case the guest's preference is for something different from the bedding provided. It is important to have a sheet and a light blanket as an alternative to a duvet. Many guests find even light quilts too hot.

When it comes to décor it needs to be neither too feminine nor too masculine. What it cannot be is childlike. You may hear 'horror' stories from guests who have gone to a Bed & Breakfast only to find themselves sleeping with pictures of fairies, and 'Miranda's Room' on the door. Guests want to feel that the room they are staying in is theirs for the duration, so unless their name is Miranda and they are 8 years old this room won't achieve it for them.

Floors should be carpeted or have rugs to help absorb noise and keep the room warmer in winter. It is very important that your window coverings, whether they are curtains or blinds, give total darkness in daylight. Your guests will probably want to sleep in and you need to ensure they can do so with ease.

You need bedside lights on both sides of the bed and plenty of accessible power points to cater for everything people travel with. Don't hide power points under the bed or behind furniture. Don't use double adaptors – they are extremely dangerous (see Chapter 9). All guest bedrooms should have a source of heating, with clear directions if needed.

Guest bedrooms should, ideally have locks on their doors. If your guests are staying for more than one night then they will want to keep personal effects in their room. They may feel they can't if there is no lock on the door and other guests can access their space.

> **TIP**
>
> Some B&Bs have a small table and chairs for two in the guest bedrooms.

As for furniture, the most important piece, other than a bed, is a wardrobe – for those rooms without fitted robes. You should supply at least five, good quality hangers per guest, definitely not the bent-wire variety!

Bedside tables are important, with a tall boy or shelves for folded items. We would recommend a chair, and a desk is often appreciated – pens and notepaper are a nice addition. Don't forget the waste paper basket in every room. An adequate mirror is also essential.

TIP
A chocolate on your guest pillows is a nice touch.

TIP
Have a list of items that are available for guests who may have left theirs at home, for example, toothbrush, toothpaste, nail file, comb, and aspirin, etc, for purchase, if necessary, or to just give them on request.

When it comes to extras – think of everything you would like in the perfect bedroom and try to provide it. A jug of water or bottle of mineral water and glasses is always appreciated. Mints are good. Tissues are essential.

Candles are a great idea and a good way to help create a romantic mood. Mini CD players are also appreciated. If you wanted to go all out you could provide guest robes, a must when guests have to go out of their room to access the bathroom.

Some people also appreciate facilities to make their own coffee and tea in their room.

HOME OFFICE

It is a good idea to set up a **home office**. You will need a space where you can deal with your paperwork, set up a computer, a facsimile and any other equipment you might need. The tax system requires you to keep precise records of your business activities and it is a great idea to have a dedicated room in which to do this. Your financial consultant will be able to advise whether or not there is a tax benefit here, but there may be.

How and where you place your office is a personal choice. We suggest that you do not put this equipment in your bedroom. Your B&B will invade much of your personal space and you need one room in your house that is free from work.

BUILDING AND DEVELOPMENT APPLICATIONS

Before authorities adopt a code or policy it usually goes through a process of community exposure and consultation. The problem is that most people show little interest in these things until their proposed plan is directly affected. It's always better to obtain all the information and satisfy requirements to begin with.

Approval has traditionally been granted to operate a home occupation (yourself) or a home industry (where you might employ other people). In granting this approval authorities would again consider local amenity issues. For example, is it likely to be noisy, have a lot of traffic coming and going, or incur other nuisance or environmental issues? Of course there are some informal, unapproved operations in existence, which authorities might not actively pursue, unless they get a complaint about them.

APPROVAL AND CONSTRUCTION OF B&B ACCOMMODATION

The most daunting part of starting a B&B might be dealing with your local authority. It sounds pretty simple to set aside a couple of bedrooms, advertise in the local paper and in roll the customers. But don't forget that you will probably need the approval of the local authorities before you start operations or before you know it, an officer will be knocking on your door and asking for an explanation.

Dealing with your **local authority** can either be like talking with a close friend, or your worse nightmare realised. A combination of official zeal and your ignorance can make the whole process confusing and frustrating. Suddenly the seemingly simple can become very complicated.

Usually, you will need to obtain **planning approval** for the use of the premises as a B&B plus building approval if any structural alterations or other modifications to the building are necessary. The good news is that usually you can make a combined application for both planning and building approval, which should speed up the process. In some instances the approvals, and certainly the building component, can be obtained through a private certifier.

A lot of the codes and policies are now written in a performance format, which means that authorities give you a series of objectives and some suggested ways of meeting those objectives. You have the flexibility to decide what you will do to achieve the requirements. However, you may still encounter some prescriptive requirements – which simply state what you must do. While this format removes any doubts about getting it right, it also takes away some of the opportunity for flexibility and innovation.

Sometimes you will be hard pressed persuading authorities of the merits of your vision for your individual establishment, particularly if it deviates in some way from the rules that have been set down. Appeal rights against an authority's decision may vary and become too costly and time-consuming to make your proposal viable. It would be much better to negotiate as much as possible in the initial stages.

You need to be aware that different parts of a building can have different classifications depending on the use of the individual parts. This can have important implications for the final classification of a building and the required type of construction.

Fire safety

As distinct from your normal house, you would be required to install a system of hard-wired **smoke alarms** in every guest bedroom and in hallways associated with guest bedrooms. If there is no hallway, smoke alarms would need to be installed in areas between guest bedrooms and the remainder of the building, and between each storey. The smoke alarms in hallways and areas outside of guest bedrooms will also be required to incorporate a light to be activated by the smoke alarm, or alternatively the smoke alarms can be wired to activate existing hallway lighting to assist evacuation of the occupants in the event of a fire.

Fire blankets should be of a size to meet the expected risk. Your local fire brigade, fire authority or specialist fire-fighting supply and installation companies should be contacted and they will guide you in your selection and installation of both fire extinguishers and fire blankets.

If you are required to provide fire safety measures and facilities, such as smoke alarms, evacuation lighting, portable fire extinguishers and fire blankets, there will be regular inspections to verify that these measures are in place, being maintained and are capable of operation at an acceptable standard that will afford the occupants of the building the required level of fire safety. It is a requirement of the fire authority, and certainly in your own interest to limit liability, to have fire safety measures inspected by an appropriately qualified person who can certify that the fire safety measures are capable of working properly.

Depending on the nature, extent and location of any additions or alterations that you might want to carry out on your building, the authority may also require you to upgrade the fire protection between your building, any associated structures on your land and adjoining properties. This will depend on the existing and proposed separation between the buildings and property boundaries.

Of necessity, this information is of a general nature only and may not be directly applicable to individual circumstances, in which case individuals should seek expert advice. Intending Bed & Breakfast owners will need to check the relevant legislation and its application at the time of any proposed development.

ENERGY AND THE BED & BREAKFAST

If you need to build extra accommodation for your B&B or Guesthouse, the following energy-saving points need to be carefully considered. There is usually little additional cost for alterations to be energy efficient, but the resulting improvements in running cost and comfort are well worth the effort.

The climate in the United Kingdom, Ireland, the Channel Islands and the Isle of Man can vary quite considerably and often very swiftly.

In winter, with the sun predominantly low in the southern sky, the longest wall of the house should face towards the south to receive the maximum exposure to the winter sunshine, providing free winter heat. Allowing natural light into your home instead of turning on lights cuts running costs considerably. In summer some shading may be required so that furniture is not damaged and curtains do not fade.

To make the most of the free heat, the rooms that require the most comfort should be located on the southern side of the home. These include: the kitchen, playroom, sitting room, dining room and any other room where comfort is needed during waking hours e.g. guest bedrooms without the use of a sitting room. Other rooms that do not require as much comfort during this time can be located on the north or east, for example most bedrooms and spare rooms.

Consider the location of anything that could obstruct the winter sun from entering the home. This could include trees, neighbouring buildings or hills. Opportunities for winter sun entry to the new home or new additions need to be maximised.

Open plan designs might look good, but can create many problems. The house should be designed with zones that can be closed off from each other. This is mainly to reduce the extent of heating, but will give an added advantage of providing both visual and noise privacy. Staircases are notorious for causing difficulty with heating and need to have doors to separate them from heated areas.

An airlock entry has two sets of doors in the foyer, the outer doors and a second inner set about two metres apart. This will allow entry to the home without allowing large amounts of heat to be lost in winter.

Double-glazing and other improved forms of glazing can reduce conductive heat flow by more than 50%. Triple glazing is apparently to be made compulsory in the near future.

Internal building materials with high thermal mass can store large amounts of heat without causing a rapid temperature change throughout the day. These materials include a concrete slab on the ground, internal walls of brick, stone, concrete block, mud brick, rammed earth, to mention a few. By adding thermal mass into the south facing living areas, the home can be kept warmer in winter, therefore reducing the amount of additional heating required.

Heat is lost or gained through six main areas in the house, the roof and ceilings, walls, windows, floors and through draughts. To maintain comfort within the building, insulation should be used to control heat flow through each of these six areas. To insulate only one or two of these areas will not solve comfort problems. House design and construction are prescriptive to allow for maximum heat retention. The amount of insulation required for each locality is mentioned on the website: www.housingenergy.org.uk

Draught proofing the house is one of the simplest and cheapest methods of improving comfort throughout the year. In older houses draughts are very common under and around doors, window frames, between floor boards, between floors and walls and skirting boards, wall and ceiling ventilators, recessed down lights, chimneys without dampers, and exhaust fans without dampers, etc. By filling the gaps, less hot air will flow out of the home.

There are many other topics of energy saving that need to be addressed. These include:

◆ the use of compact fluorescent lamps and fittings

◆ insulation of hot water pipes

◆ reduced lengths of hot water pipes

◆ efficient water heaters

◆ low water use appliances such as shower heads, washing machines, dishwashers and toilets

◆ heat recovery on ventilation systems

◆ use of efficient white goods such as refrigerators, freezers, washing machines and clothes dryers

◆ energy rated electronic equipment such as TVs, video recorders, computers, printers and fax machines.

WHAT TO ASK YOUR ARCHITECT, BUILDER OR DESIGNER

If you are interested in having an energy efficient home, you should put the following questions to your architect, builder or designer.

◆ Will the house face south?

◆ Are the largest windows located on the southern side of the house?

♦ Is the appropriate level of insulation provided in the roof, the ceiling and all external walls?

♦ Can the living area be divided into separate zones, and have doors that can be closed to isolate those heated zones in the house?

♦ Is the hot water system located with the shortest pipe run to all facilities?

♦ What type of lighting will be provided in the house?

ADVICE FOR THE HOME RENOVATOR

The basic structure of your property will determine whether it is viable to renovate or not. If the house has deteriorated in the worst sense then you could be faced with re-building the house from the ground up and the cost of doing so is seldom reflected in the market value of the improved property.

If your house has already been renovated, unless your vision contains only minor changes, it can be very costly to undo someone else's work. It is often easier and less costly to start with a blank canvas.

> **TIP**
>
> If the cost of renovating your property results in a market price over and above the reasonable value of similar properties in your area, then it probably isn't worthwhile.

Renovating requires almost a Zen-like philosophy – you require patience, adaptability and a good sense of humour to endure the ongoing chaos. Keep the dream alive, the inspiration flowing, and the lines of communication wide open. And practise the art of compromise!

WHEN YOU ARE THINKING OF RENOVATING

1. View your house as four walls and a roof, taking it back to the

bare structure. Look at what you do have, and what you don't have. Look at ways to enhance what you have to achieve what you want, before resorting to demolition tactics. It may save you a fortune in the long run. Be flexible with your ideas.

2. Look around your area for houses similar to that which you would like, taking note of market value. Will it be cheaper to build elsewhere, or buy a cheaper property to renovate? Even if you are looking at a long-term investment, it is important to stay focused on market value.

3. Ask yourself what effect you are hoping to create – olde worlde, modern, rustic, oriental, practical or luxurious are just a few examples. Do your existing windows, ceiling height and any other things that cannot be changed lend themselves to this particular idea?

4. Will the furniture that you need to buy to create the finished effect fit into the room? You would be surprised how many people have ordered furniture that will not go through their doorways!

5. You must be able to see the potential of the property. Some people are better at this than others, but there are ways to learn. There is no point in listening to someone else convincing you of potential if you can't see it yourself.

6. Consult a professional before you purchase, or before you make the decision to renovate. Speak to an architect or builder, or even someone you know as a seasoned renovator, to get an understanding of the achievable and possible, and what it will cost to arrive at your dream. Unless you have a sound understanding of housing structure, get a qualified building inspection done, and include this as a condition of purchase.

7. Balance your renovations between personal requirements and general market appeal. Over specialising your property will narrow your resale market considerably.

8. Consider the layout of the house. It is much easier and cheaper to embellish the original layout of the house, than to completely reinvent the entire house.

9. Remember the most expensive part of any renovation is the labour content. The more work you can do yourself the cheaper your renovation will be.

10. To be realistic, set yourself a timeframe, and then double it. This applies to using contractors, and more so to the 'do-it-yourself' (DIY) renovator. A 'simple' job seldom is simple, and unforeseen catastrophes can occur. Furthermore the constraints of full-time work, raising a family and social commitments can see your time allocated for renovating ebb and flow – so too your enthusiasm.

11. Be careful what building company you use. Always get more than one tradesperson to advise and quote you for the work required.

12. If the work you are having carried out is on a large scale then you should consult a surveyor. Remember, you may need planning permission for some renovations. However, if you have just moved into your home you may already have had a structural survey done.

> **TIP**
>
> Before painting a complete room use a tester tin. Paint a patch on different walls, as each will reflect the colour differently.

13. Take into consideration that some renovations may require planning permission and may have to satisfy

building regulations, for example, a new roof covering. The planning department in your locality will be able to advise you.

PLANNING PERMISSION

How much you can extend the dwelling will depend on your local authority and their individual policy. It also depends on the property type you wish to alter. There can be different limits on bungalows, semi-detached, detached, end-of-terrace and terraced properties.

There is not always a need to obtain **planning permission** as some extension work and loft conversions can be done under **Permitted Development**. This allows you to build a certain amount without submitting plans. Each government or local authority has a different, and definite, policy on what meterage is acceptable.

If you don't need to get planning permission, then a **certificate of lawful development** can be issued to you. It will show that you have submitted plans and that you were legally allowed to carry out the works.

If you are building a garage then planning permission is not always needed, but once again each authority has its own policy on meterage and siting. The roof on the garage also needs to be taken into consideration, as there are different policies for pitched and flat roofs. Permitted Development is not available on all properties, such as a listed

TIP

It is a good idea to occasionally spend the night in one of your guestrooms, testing the room's appeal, the condition of the bed and your bathroom facilities. This will help you gauge the service you are offering.

building, a building near a conservation area, or new housing developments. These will all have their own set of policies.

5

Doing Your Homework

O ver the past few years, speaking to thousands of prospective Bed & Breakfast owners, I have often faced the dilemma of how to sound enthusiastic about people's prospective ventures, while still issuing a word of caution.

To many people, more than any other venture, owning and operating a Bed & Breakfast represents a romantic ideal. I see normally rational people: doctors, lawyers, business owners, teachers, policemen, process workers, about to take huge financial risks on a venture for which they have not written a **feasibility study**.

No matter what your financial or personal expectations for your new venture, it is a business and you need to treat it with the gravity it deserves. You will find it impossible to achieve the results you want without a blueprint on how you plan to get there.

This chapter gives you some advice that you may find helpful to get you started in your venture.

SCOUT'S HONOUR

If there was one piece of advice that I would give you it is to: *be prepared.* More businesses fail due to lack of planning and ongoing financial management than for any other reason.

So why don't people plan to succeed? The main reason cited is time, or the lack of it. *Make time.* This is your life or livelihood we are talking about. A few extra months planning your venture, researching the business you are thinking of entering, *will* make the difference between success and failure.

Get out your notebook and write down your answers to the following questions:

- Do you have any business experience? Write down how you believe you can use this experience in your business.

- Do you have any other experiences you can draw on? How do you believe they will help you?

- Have you spoken to an accountant, financial adviser or business consultant?

- Have you contacted your region's tourism office to get information on your area's tourism statistics? Ask them for the number of B&Bs in your area.

- Have you contacted your local authority to get their position on Bed & Breakfast?

- Have you spoken to at least five other operators about their Bed & Breakfast experience?

- Have you stayed in at least five Bed & Breakfasts? This is important so that you can test the adequacy of the bedroom and specifically the bed and the bathroom against your perceptions.

Write down the things you believe these B&Bs are doing well, and the things you believe they could improve on. Ensure that your plan addresses these issues.

◆ Why do you believe there is a demand for another Bed & Breakfast in your area? What will be your main advantage over your competitors?

◆ Have you spoken to your area's Bed & Breakfast association if there is one? Have you contacted the national office?

◆ Is your Bed & Breakfast to be a lifestyle change or a commercial venture in the stand-alone sense?

◆ Are you buying an existing business?

◆ Have you contacted your financial adviser or business adviser to help you assess the business?

◆ Have you had a building inspection?

◆ Have you determined the financial goals you have for the business?

◆ Have you discussed with your financial adviser or business consultant what effect turning your house into a business will have on your financial affairs?

◆ Have you looked at various tourism and industry publications?

◆ Have you sought the opinions of potential customers and suppliers?

◆ Have you worked out how much it will cost you to turn your house into a Bed & Breakfast? Did you get three quotes for all work you are not going to do yourself?

◆ Have you worked out a financial plan to supplement your income while you build your business?

FINANCING

In the first year of your new enterprise you should try to **finance** your venture yourself. However, if additional funding is necessary you need to ensure you contact your small business association or consultant, your bank or building society, or a financial adviser. Remember, all start-up businesses need initial seed capital and Bed & Breakfast is not an exception.

You need to take the answers to all the questions above to any meetings you have regarding finance. It will show you have done your preparation and will keep you focused.

STARTING YOUR OWN BED & BREAKFAST

So why start your Bed & Breakfast from scratch, rather than buy an existing business?

- You are not paying for goodwill or that intangible stamp the current owners have put on the property. The value of the property is one thing, the individual characteristic, if proven, is something else. Both aspects are treated separately.

- Any reputation an establishment has, has been earned. If you are selling or buying an existing Bed & Breakfast, remember that the B&B or Guesthouse name, attached to the property, can be part of the sale or purchase, or a point of negotiation.

- You don't need to spend a lot of money at once. Your capital outlay can be gradual.

- You avoid the exit and entry costs of selling and buying a property.

- You will have the satisfaction of building the business from an embryo to a living, breathing thing.

However, starting a Bed & Breakfast from scratch is not all beer and skittles.

- You will have all the set up tasks associated with starting a Bed & Breakfast, finding good suppliers, buying beds, dealing with contractors, etc.

- You will need to work in conjunction with your tourist association to build a relationship.

- You will need to live off your savings or paying job until people hear of you.

BUYING AN ESTABLISHED B&B

Is buying an established Bed & Breakfast better? No, just different. The advantages are as follows:

- There is no start-up period.

- If you are a good operator with a solid business you could have a substantial positive cash flow from the word go.

- A marketing strategy is already in place. Your business should already be listed in your area's tourism book and possibly a nationally recognised B&B guide so that you have a place in at least two popular Bed & Breakfast guides for your region.

- If purchasing, your predecessors already have an identifiable target market. This does not mean you can't change it over time, but for now you have a ready and, hopefully, loyal clientele.

- Most of the establishment decisions have been made – and as you have purchased the property it is taken for granted that you believe the decisions were the right ones. That leaves you to get on with the business of the day-to-day running of the establishment.

Are there disadvantages? Certainly.

♦ You will be investing a large amount of capital immediately. If this is to be your career then that is not such a problem, but if it is just a way to earn some extra cash, then the financial commitment could be far too large.

♦ You could be paying far too much for your prospective business. You need to determine how important the previous owner was to the business and how much return business you can expect when considering the purchase price. Look at the visitors book and assess how much the business could potentially suffer during the changeover period.

♦ You will be tying up your funds in a business that takes time to sell, if the need arises. You will be paying more than if it were just a family home. Be aware of this before making any decisions.

♦ You need to assess whether what you are paying for the furniture, en suites, china, etc, is a reasonable price.

IS IT GOING TO WORK?

In order to make sense of all the above you need to first test the viability of your proposed B&B investment by completing a **feasibility study**.

You must use the knowledge gained from completing the feasibility study as your stepping-stone to achieving your goals and aspirations. The research you need to do to make your Bed & Breakfast a success must be unique to you and your market.

If the findings in your feasibility study are positive then the assumptions can be used as a basis for your business plan. On the other hand, if the results of your study are negative, then move on.

Your feasibility study will help you to:

- decide whether you still want to enter the market
- prepare a realistic financial analysis to help you enter the industry
- help to decide whether to buy, or build a new dwelling.

Professionalism, above all, is most important. Clear thinking will reinforce the need to gather critical information in the early phase of your proposed venture and give you an insight into the level of commitment needed to succeed in this business.

Owning and operating a Bed & Breakfast is the dream of many, but you must balance that dream with the reality of owning and running a viable business. Every dream must have the structure of a plan, for your dream won't just happen. You need to develop a strategy to achieve that dream.

Your plan is an exercise to assist you in making your investment decisions. It is also a formalised analysis that can encourage meaningful discussions with your partner, family and financial advisers, and potential lenders.

The written outline of your business idea is designed to help you focus more clearly on what exactly you are planning in your B&B operation.

- How would you describe your idea to someone else?

- Do you intend to run a B&B that you would be delighted to stay in and recommend?

- ◆ Why will your proposal be different from other B&B operations?

- ◆ Why should people want to stay with you?

- ◆ What will you offer them, apart from somewhere to stay?

- ◆ In short, why will your Bed & Breakfast venture be successful?

YOUR START-UP CAPITAL COSTS

At this point you can work out just how much it will cost to put into place any alterations and improvements you want, together with the furnishings you require.

The other major start-up costs to be considered are your professional fees, eg your solicitor and accountant or financial adviser.

YOUR FINANCIAL VIABILITY

The best way to evaluate the financial viability of your proposed B&B is to focus on **net profit**.

The reason for this is that you need net profit to pay for your living expenses and your loan repayments unless you have another source of income that will subsidise these payments. Once you have established your net profit requirements, the next step is to look at the sales level required to provide you with this profit.

ESTABLISH YOUR ANNUAL SALES LEVEL

Having worked out how much net profit is required to achieve your goals, it is possible to work backwards to estimate the sales level required to produce this net profit.

It is my experience that costs of production, that is, food and provisions can usually run around 25% of trading income. Given this estimate, gross profit would represent 75% of trading income. From this 75% all operating expenses will have to be deducted.

In a commercial Bed & Breakfast enterprise, I believe that a minimum industry average of around 25% total income is an acceptable level of net profit.

This percentage can be higher, contingent on occupancy levels, and whether or not you out-source tasks like cleaning, laundry, etc.

ASCERTAIN THE REALITY OF YOUR SALES TARGET

At this stage, ask the question: 'Can guest bookings at this level be reached?' To help you in working out your ability to meet **target income levels**, construct a daily room rate income 'ready reckoner'. This is a simple way of matching room rates you select with the number of guest rooms available. However, it does not take into account your expected occupancy rate.

Your consideration is to ascertain how quickly you can convert your guest room availability and your expected occupancy rate into yearly-anticipated bed nights. Work on a 48-week per year basis.

By combining the information from these two exercises you can nominate your room rate and thus set your daily guest room income. This will enable you to estimate your occupancy rates and thereby establish your anticipated yearly bed nights, thus projecting your potential income.

> **TIP**
>
> Remember the old adage: you have to spend money to make money. Doing things on the cheap is usually a waste of your hard-earned savings.

COMMERCIAL VENTURE

The industry average occupancy rate for a well-run B&B establishment, located in an area where you can attract the corporate market mid-week and the leisure market during the weekends, ranges from 40% to 70%. Whereas, in a lifestyle situation, the average occupancy rate ranges from 20% to 60%.

MAKING A DECISION

You have now reached the stage where you can compare your potential income with the income you need if you are to match or exceed your break-even point.

If your potential income is below your break-even level, go back to your earlier work, re-evaluate your cost options, expenditures, etc. and see the effect as you re-work your calculations.

Your feasibility study is, as stated earlier, a simply formalised approach to assist you in making your investment decisions. It provides you with a facility to evaluate your options every step of the way. It will not, however, make the final decision for you. You alone can make that decision.

If your decision were simply a matter of evaluating the economic viability of your proposed B&B, then such a decision would be an easy one to make. However, there are other key factors which impact on your final decision to proceed. These non-economic factors are: your private/family lifestyle expectations, and the willingness of your partner and family to match you in your commitment to be a totally professional host.

After looking at the results of the viability of your proposal and also at the non-economic factors I have just mentioned, you may decide *not* to proceed with your Bed & Breakfast proposal. If this is the situation, then the feasibility study you have completed has still been a worthwhile exercise. It is a lot easier to withdraw at this stage than it is once your venture is actually up and running. If, however, you conclude that your venture *is* viable and that you want to proceed, then the knowledge gained from your feasibility study is invaluable and will form the basis for your business plan when you write one.

It is strongly advised that those contemplating entry into this industry obtain the companion book to the one you are now reading as it enables you to write your own feasibility study using the tables and work sheets at the back of the book.

TIP

Keep yourself up to date with short break holiday trends. This market segment is about to take off.

A Feasibility Study for Aspiring Bed & Breakfast Operators – by Stewart Whyte with Wal Reynolds – available at: www.bnb-central.com or www.howtobooks.co.uk

Part Two
How to Run Your B&B Efficiently and Successfully

6

Putting People Back in Service

S ervice. It is a word that you will hear over and over again in this chapter. Being willing and able to provide exceptional **customer service** is one of the keys to being a successful Bed & Breakfast operator.

The first section (Chapters 1–5) discussed whether you were the right sort of person to be a Bed & Breakfast host. By now we can assume that your positives outweighed your negatives. Get your answers to the questions from Chapter 1 and read them again. Are your answers the same?

There is no doubt that having had some prior experience in a service industry will stand you in good stead when running a Bed & Breakfast. But if you have not had the advantage of this experience all is not lost. You have been a consumer your whole adult life. Take some time to think about the best service that you have ever received when on holiday. What made it so good? What about the worst service? What was bad about it?

Service is a strange entity. If is often about perception. To one customer your behaviour may seem cloying and intrusive, to the next, receiving exactly the same service, you might seem remote and cold. The level of service is the same, but your guest has perceived it differently. Often the perception of good service isn't about how guests feel about you at all. Freshly ground coffee first thing in the morning, the morning paper outside their bedroom door, freshly baked scones for afternoon tea – these are things that can make up good service in your guests' minds.

In this chapter we are going to focus on how you can ensure all the dealings you have with your guests are consistent and special for them.

COMMUNICATING WITH PROSPECTIVE GUESTS

My name is...

Your name is an integral part of making your guests feel at home. All of your interactions with your guests, whether on the telephone, by email, or in person should be personal and nothing will get this across as quickly as your using your guest's name and their using yours. Introduce yourself by your first name and ask your guest if they would mind if you used theirs. People stay at B&Bs because they like the feeling of intimacy and 'home' that they represent. Using your first name, and theirs, is an easy way to give your guests an identity, and make them feel part of your family – even if it's only for a day.

Telephone and fax

Ideally, you will want to invest in the installation of a separate line from that of your home phone. For a small price you can ensure that you know that the call is for your business and you can answer accordingly. It also allows other members of the household to make personal calls without fear of missing a booking. It is suggested that if you have young children you prevent them from answering the 'business' phone. If you are going out you can either divert your **business phone** to your mobile (another necessity) or switch on your answering machine.

For those of you without a fax modem, a **fax** machine is an essential tool, given that you may wish to send your guest a sketch map showing how to find your B&B.

Answering the phone

Answer the phone with the name of your establishment and your name. Smile when speaking on the phone, it shines through and you can hear it.

Always sound friendly, relaxed and courteous – you have already acknowledged you are a people person so this should be very easy.

You need to ensure that you have your **reservation diary** and a **pen** by the telephone. You don't want to have to ask your caller to wait while you get organised – it doesn't leave a good impression. It is a great idea to ask questions of your caller so you can determine things that may be of interest of them and build some rapport with them as soon as possible. Note the kind of language a guest uses, so that you can match the style when you are talking to them later. By matching your caller's voice tone you will make them feel comfortable with you. They will also give you much more useful information if they feel you empathise with them.

Most of all you need to remember that much of your business will be won or lost by the information you present to your customer over the telephone or email and how you present it.

TIP

Learn to turn every enquiry into a booking, and smile!

Email

It is a very different world from even five years ago. Over the past five years the **internet** has exploded and the reality is that much of the communication you have with potential guests will be over the Internet. Over 22% of internet users have used it to book accommodation over the last 12 months. This is a statistic that is destined to grow.

For potential international and corporate guests, the Internet and email will be the main form of communication. It has the enormous advantage of being cheap and comprehensive, not to mention visual.

Ensure that the tone of your email is friendly yet professional. You need to check emails regularly and follow up any inquiries promptly. Check your spelling and grammar as even something as minor as this can deter some potential guests. They may believe that if you care so little for your business that you did not take the time to run a spell check you might not care about the details of their stay.

Questions

As much of your business will be won or lost by what you say over the phone, or on email, there are a number of commonly asked questions that you should have the answers to.

The following is a list that you might like to start with. As people ask other questions write the answer down and put them with this list in the front of your reservation diary.

How can we reach you?

You need to be able to provide detailed **directions** on how your guest can reach you by car, public transport or walking, particularly if you are down unnamed lanes or a little out of the way. You might also give some idea of travelling time and distance. Ask potential guests for their address, fax or email so you can send them a map. Directions should assume your guests are arriving with a tired, hungry family on a dark, wet night. Your directions should be so good that they are able to find you without any assistance. If you have specific parking instructions – for example, some local authorities will not allow on-street parking – you will need to be able to provide this information as well. They may even ask you to detail how close you are to local attractions with instructions how they might get there. Check in and check out times for your B&B are also important.

Once your guests confirm the booking you will need to pinpoint their arrival time as closely as possible, so you can ensure you are prepared.

RESERVATION DETAILS

You need to be able to present room rates and feature details as a friendly sales person would. This is your chance to win the guest's business. Now is your opportunity to advise:

- how far ahead you need booking confirmation
- availability
- minimum night restrictions (2 nights on a weekend, for example),
- deposit details (how much, refundable or non refundable)
- cancellation penalties.

At this initial stage, you will also need to advise how you accept payment – cash, cheque, credit cards, etc.

🏠 🏠 Ask your bank for the application forms that would ultimately enable you to process MasterCard, Visa and Bankcard. Many of your guests will expect this payment option (see Chapter 7 for more details).

(see Chapter 7 for more details).

> **TIP**
>
> Offer to help plan a local itinerary. This can be done initially in your welcoming letter or upon your guests arrival.

FEATURES AND BENEFITS

You will often be asked by potential guests to provide the **features and benefits** of your establishment: the size of your rooms; any theme rooms you might have, eg decorated on a nationality theme; bed configuration; whether or not the room is serviced daily; whether the bathrooms are shared or if you have en suites; if you have a spa bath in any of the rooms. This is your opportunity to promote your Bed & Breakfast. You need to be able to talk about the meals you provide, whether they eat with you or privately, you may even be asked to provide some sample menus.

You may be asked about alcohol, whether it can be bought nearby, or if it is 'bring your own'.

Some guests, especially from abroad, may ask whether there are cooking facilities they can use, a small kitchenette, or BBQ in summer. Any extras you provide such as laundry facilities, irons, hairdryers, phone lines, Internet access, etc., also need to be detailed here. If you have special packages for honeymoons, corporate clients, special school events or special interests, now is the time to offer to tell your potential guest about them.

CHILDREN, PETS AND SMOKING

By now you will have determined your policy on these issues and you need to detail these to all prospective bookings. It is better your guests know your stance now rather than having a possible misunderstanding when they arrive.

> **TIP**
> Always tell your guest at the time of booking that there is a no-smoking policy.

SPECIAL NEEDS

Guests may ask you whether you have **facilities for the disabled** and you will need to be able to advise them about any modifications you have made. If you don't have appropriate facilities (such as wheelchair access) you need to tell them. **Dietary specialities** are another thing you may be asked to cater for. If you provide an evening meal you may wish to ask at the point of reservation whether any of the party have any food restrictions, so you can plan in advance.

LOCAL ACTIVITIES AND ATTRACTIONS

You need to know *everything* about your local area, as guests will have the expectation that you are their local guide to the area.

> **TIP**
> Be part of your guests' holiday by being available for general conversation and helpful advice.

Sell the best parts of your locality to your potential guests as this could sway them in your direction and also in the duration of their stay. You also need to be able to provide details of great places to eat in your area. Guests may ask you to send menus of local pubs and restaurants or even make bookings for them.

WRITTEN CORRESPONDENCE

If there is enough time a **letter** should follow up any telephone inquiries about your establishment, preferably the next day. This letter needs to be neatly presented and on a letterhead. As with email, correct spelling is paramount.

The letter should not give the impression of being a standard form, even if is. Try to personalise the letter with some information that your caller asked for over the phone and use their first names, as well as yours.

If you are replying to particular questions, answer these questions specifically, not with 'our brochure is enclosed', although by all means enclose your brochure as well.

Once people have booked a room, follow up their booking with a written confirmation and a map. It is details like this that will make a difference.

HERE AT LAST

Now is the moment you have been waiting for – the moment you come face to face with your guests and welcome them to your Bed & Breakfast. Again, you need to do your best to put your guests at ease immediately so they feel they are at their home away from home. Introduce yourself by your first name and if you know your guest's first name, use it with permission, as it will help put everyone at ease.

Ideally, when the guests arrive, and after they have freshened up, show them around and suggest that they come and join you for a quality drink and some freshly baked goodies. The morning/

afternoon tea has multiple purposes:

- It will allow you to get to know one another.

- You can find out what they intend to do while staying in your area and it will allow you the opportunity to offer suggestions.

- It will give you the opportunity to show off your baking skills. The provision of a hot breakfast and freshly baked food are cited as two of the main reasons people like to stay in Bed & Breakfasts.

When dealing with your guests there are a number of things you can use that will help you to achieve the perception of fantastic service.

BE ATTENTIVE

You need to appear interested in what your guests say. Remember the information they are giving you will help you make their stay special. You do, however, need to learn how to extricate yourself from a clinging guest without leaving them thinking you don't have time for them.

> **TIP**
>
> Guests want to be nurtured not smothered!

Your body language

Try to match **body language** in a subtle way. Face your guests directly. Don't fiddle or fidget – it gives the impression of boredom and nervousness. You want your guests to feel you are both comfortable and interested.

Maintain eye contact

The majority of people will believe you are not interested in them if you do not have eye contact with them. They may also mistrust your sincerity.

Match your tone of voice to your meaning

You need to ensure that you sound like you mean what you say, and say what you mean. A mismatch will be evident to your listener. Try to modulate your voice and match the tone to your guest's.

Build rapport

From the first contact with your guest, take a few minutes to build rapport. This is easy to do with people you know or like, it takes real professionalism to achieve it with people you don't know or like.

You need to learn how to do it with conscious skill. The easiest way to do this is with body language. Be subtle here, matching the angle and position of the head and torso and only approximating the position of the arms and legs, as it is these that will make your mirroring obvious if you imitate your guests too closely.

Note the language your guests use and try to use similar words, matching the tone and speed of their voice.

These may sound like very simple suggestions, but they have remarkably powerful effects.

Try them out first on people other than your guests, so that when you use these skills on your guests you can also pay attention to what they are saying until your rapport-building skills become automatic.

DRESS FOR SUCCESS

Your outward appearance is a personification of how your guests will view your establishment. If you dress well and look after yourself, your guests will believe you take the same care of your establishment. You need to ensure you are always dressed in a dressy casual style. For men, that might be a pair of slacks with a casual shirt. For women it is something you would be comfortable going to lunch in. Your hair should be clean and well groomed. Your nails should be clean and well trimmed.

For women, make up should be subtle. Everyone needs to ensure their breath is fresh and they have an absence of body odour.

If you are serving dinner we would suggest a change of clothes. You want to give your guests a bit of 'theatre'.

Always be aware of your attire. Primarily, it is the male partner we are concerned with here. Don't be caught out! The suitably attired female partner in the Bed & Breakfast venture may need to race down to the local shop to get something, and her partner, up to his eyes in gardening, says, 'If the guests arrive while you are out I will look after them'. A nice thought, but is this casual approach going to appear professional in the eyes of a paying guest?

When cleaning, wear clothes that are easy to launder, neat and do not show the dirt. Your shoes should have rubber soles in the interest of safety. Remove any jewellery when cooking or cleaning as it may be damaged by the cleaning agents.

SMOKING

No matter what your decision is regarding smoking, you personally should not smoke inside in front of guests. You should never smoke while working. Nothing is more offensive than one hand on a vacuum cleaner while the other is holding a lit cigarette. It is all about professionalism.

BEHAVIOUR

This is where your people skills come in. If your guests look like they want to be left alone, then respect their privacy. If on the other hand your guests want to chat, then remember it's in your time and subsequently you may need to determine the duration. This is a skill you will need to master.

You need always to work as quietly as possible. When guests come to stay with you, they are there to relax. They will often read, sleep in, or just rest. You want to minimise any negative impact you may have on them.

When it comes to conversation there are a few golden rules.

♦ Never talk about religion, sex or politics until it is safely established that these topics are acceptable. Don't be baited into getting into these topics with your guests. Such discussions usually end badly.

♦ Be friendly and nice, but don't over-host. Present an aura of friendliness that doesn't tip over into familiarity. Be available to your guests for helpful advice.

♦ After breakfast is a great time to offer some suggestions about things to see and do in your area.

♦ Never speak to your guests about your personal problems or concerns. Your guests have sometimes come away to have a break from their problems – never burden them with yours.

TIP

Recognise your guests' need for privacy.

STAFF

All the following information should apply to any staff you hire – from the casual who comes in once a fortnight to help clean, to a full time chef, if you are the proprietor of a larger establishment.

Do not rush into **hiring staff**, for in the first few years of a non-established Bed & Breakfast you will gain considerable cost savings if you can do much of the work yourself. It is also much easier to manage staff if you have the experience of doing their type of work.

If you decide you need to hire labour you need to consider the following:

◆ Work out a job description with clear duties and expectations.

◆ Ensure that your employees understand exactly what is expected of them and that you will be performance managing them to those criteria.

◆ Obtain a copy of any union agreement or award from the appropriate union body.

◆ Develop a win-win agreement where performance will be monitored regularly and rewarded appropriately. If you need to performance manage you will then have an appropriate forum in which to do so. The ability to retain employees will serve you in good stead for the future.

◆ Ask your staff to bring **feedback** to their performance appraisals – from you or your partner, from a fellow staff member and from a guest or supplier.

◆ Train your staff regularly on different areas of your business. Everyone should have training on customer service and occupational health and safety.

◆ Hold a weekly staff meeting for general news and information and for everyone to have their say. Use this forum to update your staff on your business goals and performance. This is also a great time to recognise and reward employees who are performing well.

ENTERING A GUEST BEDROOM

Even though it may be a room in your house, while guests are paying for accommodation, it is their room. There may be a time, however, during your guests' stay that you may need to enter their bedroom, to make their beds, etc.

To avoid any possible embarrassment to either party you should follow a few simple and easy rules.

Always knock on the door and wait for an answer. If after 20 seconds there is no reply knock again. If again no answer you should call out a greeting 'Good morning/afternoon' and enter the room. If you are there to clean the room and your guests are still there, ask them if they wish you to come back later. Don't ever knock on a room that has a 'Do not disturb' sign displayed. It is a good idea to provide these in all rooms for your guests' use – it helps you as a signal on whether or not they wish to be disturbed.

Some B&Bs advise their guests that the host's normal procedure is to stay out of their room unless the guest has a specific need that requires someone to go in there.

GUEST BEHAVIOUR

You have some liberties here if your Bed & Breakfast is also your home. You have the right to set some rules such as how much alcohol can be consumed, noise levels, etc. How you monitor this, and to what length you wish to go is a more difficult question.

The main reason you may want to comment on a guest's behaviour is if it is disturbing you or other guests, if you suspect damage to your property, or if you suspect some illegal activity is occurring.

If you have to confront your guests about their **behaviour** you should:

◆ Do so in person, and in private. If the problem is occurring in the guest bedroom approach your guest there. Don't enter the room, but conduct your conversation at the door.

◆ Try not to sound judgemental. Instead, gently advise your guest of the nature of the complaint and the suggested behaviour. Thank them for their time and excuse yourself.

If the guest's behaviour does not improve you need to follow up your concern with the guest. Explain to the guest that it is your policy that the comfort of all of your guests is paramount, and that one individual guest cannot disturb the peace of others. Ask for the guest to show consideration to their fellow guests.

In most cases this will be enough, however in rare cases you may have to ask the guest to leave. If they refuse you will need to contact the police. If you have the unhappy experience of this happening you need to ensure that you are discreet in your handling of the affair, and keep the disturbance of any other guests to a minimum.

If on entering a room you find damage to your property you should make a report of it and add it to your guest's bill. If the guest has already checked out you should forward an account of the damage to the offender.

SEXUAL HARASSMENT

It rarely occurs in the Bed & Breakfast environment, but you may, at some time, be the victim of **sexual harassment.** Sexual harassment is an unwanted sexual advance, a request for sexual favours, or any unwelcome conduct of a sexual nature. Sexual harassment is not mutual attraction between two parties. Sexual harassment is against the law.

Under the Sex Discrimination Act, management has a duty to prevent sexual harassment and you, the employer, may be responsible if it occurs to one of your employees unless all reasonable steps have been taken to prevent it.

If you are being harassed you need to make your objections very clear to your harasser. Make a diary note about it. If your harasser tries to make fun of you or acts unaware, repeat your objection clearly and your wish that it will cease immediately. If it continues and the harasser is in your employ, that is sufficient reason for dismissal. You must contact the police if it is a criminal offence such as rape. That said, we have not heard of one case around the world where a staff member of a Bed and Breakfast has been the victim of any form of assault by a guest.

NEIGHBOURS

Your **neighbours'** feelings about your Bed & Breakfast venture are going to be a key to your success. They are going to be near you every day of the year, not just during the fleeting stays of your visitors.

They are not getting any financial benefit from your venture so you need to ensure that you minimise any impact on them. There are a few things you can do to make this relationship easier:

- Make sure that your guests are aware of any rights of way and do not block your neighbours' access.

- Make sure your guests know where your property ends and your neighbour's property begins.

- Try to ensure that you follow disturbance rules regarding noise.

- Take the time to get to know your neighbours.

- Give them one of the treats you make your guests occasionally, or invite them in for coffee. Little gestures like this will pay off.

COMPLAINTS

It is human nature to complain. Occasionally you are going to have a customer who believes your best is not good enough. You need to use these complaints to your advantage; they are valuable feedback, which will enable you to refine your product. You will find that very few people will complain, but if you investigate you may find that other guests feel the same way. Every complaint will be different, but you need to ensure that your establishment has a procedure for dealing with complaints, which everyone understands.

A correctly handled complaint can actually increase goodwill in your business. If you don't train your employees in dealing with complaints you could in effect serve to amplify the problem to a level that could substantially damage your business.

The following are some guidelines you should consider in your handling of complaints.

Don't underestimate the power of listening

Look your guest directly in the eye, face them and listen to what they have to say. It is often a good idea to offer your guest a seat. Sit down as well; you do not want to seem intimidating.

Do not take the complaint personally

Your guest will often be upset with a situation, not with you. Speak quietly. This works very well if your guest is speaking loudly. The guest's volume will be unconsciously lowered to match yours.

Apologise

A statement like 'I am sorry you feel that way' does not admit fault but acknowledges your guest's feelings. Do not make excuses or trivialise the complaint. The customer only wants to know you are taking the grievance seriously. Avoid being drawn into a right and wrong argument. *Even if you win the argument, you will end up the loser if you make the guest feel trivialised.*

Deal with the complaint in a timely manner

If you need to investigate the matter further, ask your guest's permission to do so. While you are investigating offer your guest a cup of coffee.

If the complaint is about a meal, replace it, no questions asked. Bad food will leave a bad taste in your guest's mouth in more ways than one.

Keep control of the situation

The more unreasonable and irate your guest may be the more

important it is that you stay cool, calm and collected. You need to look at the encounter as a challenge – *who can be the calmest, wins.* Adopt a constructive businesslike attitude. This will help move the sphere of the encounter from emotion to reason.

Never patronise or humiliate a guest

Patronising or humiliating guests can have disastrous results, and in the event that the mistake was yours or a member of your staff, you will be the one who will be humiliated.

Follow up

Ensure that your guest was happy with your decision. Sometimes we believe we have settled a matter appropriately, only to find out, too late, that the guest was not at all happy. You must clarify the situation for mutual satisfaction.

The next step

Fixing complaints in the short term is one thing, fixing the long-term problem is just as important. In order to analyse complaints you need to put yourself in your guest's shoes and then ask yourself the following questions.

- Is the complaint justified? Is it a disagreement with your establishment's policy or with a matter of principle?

- Is the complaint genuine? Is it the result of a unique situation, a personality clash, or a genuinely difficult customer? (Trust us – they are rare but they do exist.)

- Is it the first time you have heard the complaint, or is this complaint a frequent one?

- Is it a problem with a person or a system?

◆ Is it a trivial matter that has grown in size or intensity because of neglect?

After analysing the answers to the above you need to set up a process to prevent it from happening again. If the complaint was about a person, other than yourself, you need to address the problem immediately. Use the same principles of listening and empathy that you used with your guest. Ensure, however, your staff member understands the importance of guest happiness in your business.

THE IMPORTANCE OF FEEDBACK

As discussed before, feedback, both positive and negative, can be the most important tool in the ongoing success of your business. Most guests won't express dissatisfaction directly to you, but would be most happy to fill in a **questionnaire**.

You can leave the questionnaire in the bedroom, accompanied by a thank you letter and a stamped, self-addressed envelope. Your guest is given the option of leaving the questionnaire or posting it, or sending it by email after their stay. This action will demonstrate you are interested in their considered comments.

> **TIP**
>
> You might consider a quarterly, one page newsletter that points out forthcoming events in your area that, from knowledge gained from past guests, would be of interest.

As an incentive for filling in the questionnaire, you could offer your guests a bonus, such as 'Stay three nights, get one free', and advise them of cooking schools, fishing weekends, gourmet dinners, family fortnights, etc. that they may wish to take advantage of.

HELEN'S PLACE GUEST QUESTIONNAIRE

As part of our ongoing commitment for excellence, we ask that you fill in the spaces beside the questions and leave it here, or post it back to us using the reply paid envelope. It should be mentioned that the contents are for research purposes only and will remain confidential.

As a token of our appreciation, we will place your name in our annual lucky draw for a free, two-night stay in our Bed & Breakfast. The results of the draw will be mailed to you at the end of this year.

Name and Address:_____

_____ Telehone no:_____

Was your stay with us up to your expectations? Y N (please circle)

Please explain why_____

_____

Was Helen's Place easy to find? Y N (please circle)

How do you believe we could improve Helen's Place?_____

_____

What was the purpose of your visit in our area?_____

_____

Have you any plans to come our way again? Y N (please circle)

Will you recommend Helen's Place to your friends? Y N (please circle)

Would you be interested in receiving Helen's Place Gazette, our quarterly newsletter? Y N (please circle)

Thank you, and please don't forget to leave this or post it in the envelope provided to: PO BOX 0000, Your Town. Post Code. Helen & Warren Smith.

You can also advise them of events in your local community they might be interested in and any changes you may have made to your establishment (the addition of a spa bath in one of the bedrooms, for example).

Checklist

- Make sure your phone is manned as much as possible as most guests want to speak to the proprietor of a Bed & Breakfast, at some stage, before they book. How you conduct yourself during that conversation will often determine whether or not you clinch the booking. Don't let your personal worries intrude into your telephone manner. You must always sound as if you haven't a care in the world, and you're the warmest, most caring and hospitable person imaginable. That doesn't mean that you have to pour on the syrup with a ladle – insincerity will work against you as much as being grumpy. Just be pleasant, ready to please, and – be yourself.

- If you have to set the **answering machine**, and most of us do at some time, *do* record a message that reflects your character. *Don't* leave some morbid tone that would be more appropriate for a funeral parlour! If you can, make it mildly humorous, or something that reflects the service you offer. If you're not confident you can record a good message – get someone who can!

- Try to think of ways you can supplement your Bed & Breakfast income. If you have a historic house perhaps you can open it for public inspection. Garden open days are also very popular. If your garden is your pride and joy you may be able to take part in your community's open programme each a year. You can charge admission, which you can pour back into maintaining the garden. If you have a beautiful front parlour you may be able to hire it out to community groups for their monthly meetings.

- You may need to be resourceful in the first few years to build both positive word of mouth acknowledgement and for your income generation.

7

Day-to-Day Operations

S o your guests are here. You have your people skills off pat. You have established a business model that works for you. What you now need to do is look at the best way to run your business day to day. You need to establish systems that will allow you to enjoy your new lifestyle, and provide your guests with a fantastic holiday experience.

BOOKINGS

Chapter 6 covered the things you will need to communicate to prospective guests over the phone and the Internet. What you need to now think about are the **bookings** themselves, primarily how you are going to record them.

For those of you starting your own Bed & Breakfast we would suggest you start with a **diary**. Divide each day into the number of rooms you have available. As you take bookings you should record the following information in the appropriate room:

- ◆ The date you took the booking.
- ◆ The arrival and departure date of your guest.
- ◆ The guest's name, address and phone number.
- ◆ Deposit information.
- ◆ Any comments, such as particular dietary requirements, estimated time of arrival, etc.

We would also suggest you set up a **reservation chart** at the front of the diary, or on the wall of your office, near your phone. This will help you see at a glance if you have rooms free on a requested date.

With both the chart and the diary it is a good idea to make your reservations in pencil, in case alterations are made. Don't forget to block out days that you will not be taking guests on the chart and in the diary. For later reference place the reason next to these 'time off' days, for example holidays, family time, repairs, maintenance, etc. Any chance bookings, that is, guests who arrive without a reservation, should also be added to both the chart and the diary.

TIP

Have a cancellation policy and be prompt with refunds if applicable.

The other part of the booking is the **deposit**. We would suggest you take at least 25% as a deposit. Many Bed & Breakfasts are making these deposits non-refundable. You must specify this at the time of booking. For holidays and other busy times we suggest you take a larger deposit. Another good idea is to have minimum stays for events and long weekends, for example minimum three nights stay. This will ensure your occupancy is high and you don't miss out on other bookings during peak periods.

BOOKINGS AND THE INTERNET

We have discussed above about the most basic way to record your bookings. However, in this new technical age, with many travellers utilising the **Internet** for bookings, we wanted to know how this might affect Bed & Breakfasts. We asked Gideon and Sara Stanley of Grace Software Inc, a recognised leader in reservation system design for Bed & Breakfasts, the following questions:

Question: Why does a B&B operator need to have a reservation system?

Answer: The property owner can manage reservations, monitor marketing efforts and also make rooms available on the internet for booking. For this you need an end-to-end reservation system. The reservation software, which runs on the property's own PC, is the centre for all these activities.

The 'back end' system

Some small property owners who have not yet bought into reservation software mistakenly think it's a matter of transferring paper reservation information to a computer system. An effective reservation system offers much more, including occupancy and income reports, the ability to monitor your marketing efforts and to store important details about your guests, which is readily available any time they return for a stay.

The 'front end' system

In recent years, the Internet has contributed to the marketing potential of a fully computerised, reservation system. It has provided small- and medium-sized properties with the same opportunity and power as the larger properties. Now small property managers can regulate their online reservations with the sophistication of the large hotel chains.

Question: Why is accessible accommodation availability important to a global reservation facility?

Answer: B&Bs and Guesthouses don't have enough business guests to justify a designated terminal and the costly links to global airline reservation systems like Sabre or Apollo. With individual accommodation providers having access to a global reservation facility plus booking engine, guests searching for places to stay on the internet have access to both your reservation and property information. Providing immediate information about availability is critical for a small property. Often the first question a potential guest will ask concerns dates and availability. By offering this information on a web site, the guest's first concern is handled instantly and they can proceed by filling out a reservation form. Because of the internet, your property can now provide this immediate availability information, traditionally available only through the costly Sabre systems.

Question: What are the other advantages of having such an integrated system?

Answer: Marketing information at your fingertips. As new guests arrive at your property, you can record their referral source and preferences. At a later date, this information can easily be compiled into a report that indicates which marketing venues are most effective, and perhaps how they are effective, eg certain packages or rooms.

What are your guests' preferences? For what kind of occasion do they visit your property? Knowing the answers to these questions better positions you to attract those guests for many return visits. In a reservation management system you can create categories to track your guests' interests, as well as store specific notes that pertain to one individual guest. On their return visit, they will be pleasantly surprised at how well you remember them and their references! Storing such vital information helps build lasting customer relationships.

Question: Why is your software a good option?

Answer: Easy InnKeeping is an end-to-end reservation system. It is software designed with the internet in mind. The Internet is increasingly becoming a source of new referrals for small lodging properties. Linking the marketing power of the internet with a software program like Easy InnKeeping, gives the property owner the ability to realise their marketing potential, while retaining control over their own room inventory. Offering availability information via the Internet is easily managed from the software program itself, which operates from your own PC. For those properties interested in real-time reservations via the Internet, this option is also available.

Online reservations with availability options

Why is it important to show availability information to Internet surfing guests? The Internet is a medium of information, and studies show that the more information your web site provides to the potential guest, the more likely they are to continue 'browsing' or 'visiting' your site. Answering the question: 'Do you have availability?' is often the first step towards making a reservation. You may wonder how to display this information on your site and keep it up to date. From within the software program, you can choose to display availability information on your web site and/or in large directories.

After guests search for availability, their reservation request is sent securely to the Easy InnKeeping software. You will receive an 'alert' that prompts you to check your 'inbox'. All reservation details are displayed – just click 'save' and email the confirmation.

Customisation

The developers of Easy InnKeeping realise that the B&B industry varies from one location to another and changes with the times. For properties that have very specific needs, Easy InnKeeping can be customised to fit so that it works for you.

To better understand the value of having your B&B online for reservations, consider this: one third of Internet use today is travel related as more people use this medium to confirm their holiday plans and arrangements.

By displaying your Bed & Breakfast on a reservation system your property is made visible to potential guests from any part of the world. The beauty of online systems is twofold: Bed & Breakfast operators need not always be attending the phones, and travellers can have a confirmed reservation printed from their web browser without picking up the phone to make a call.

The more professional online reservation networks normally charge a flat fee for bookings made through the system.

GUEST REGISTRATION

Guests may not have any obligation to provide you with their permanent address, but we would suggest you ask for this, not least for the database you can then create to use for marketing at a later date.

Up until a few years ago an exercise book was sufficient for this purpose, but every year the level of professionalism in this industry is rising and it is this professionalism your guests will remember. They don't want to necessarily check in as if they were staying in a hotel, but an exercise book is not really good enough.

So what are the options? There are two main forms of **registration**. One is the use of a **guest register** and the other is the **individual registration form** or card.

Guest register

This is a bound book, divided into columns, which your guests fill in upon arrival.

Guests from overseas need to fill out the country of residence and passport number and in some cases, their next destination. In this situation you will need to sight your guest's passport.

In some regions there is a legal requirement for larger establishments to keep a record of the full name and nationality of all guests over the age of 16 years. In this situation records must be kept for a minium of twelve months. We suggest you contact your local authority about the legal requirements in your area. The Data Protection Act 1998 spells out your responsibilities in regard to the use of information.

The guest register is popular because all the details are in one place and in chronological order, making it easy for referral, and it is inexpensive as each guest only takes up one line in the register. The downsides are that it can become tatty from overuse, illegible if guests make mistakes, and indiscreet, as your guests can easily see the personal details of other guests.

Individual registration form or card

The individual registration form or card performs the same functions as a register. It is more expensive than a register as each guest has an individual card or form, but you can generate these forms easily from your computer. This format is discreet as no one sees the form, but you and your guest. It is neat, if a guest makes a mistake you can provide a new one and it can be filed easily. It also has space for both you and your guest to make comments (dietary, special needs, etc), which can be valuable information for later visits.

> **TIP**
>
> Make sure your customers are satisfied even if you can't personally help them. For example, if you have no available accommodation on the given night refer them to someone who can help.

INSURANCE

We asked people in the insurance industry for their comments and recommendations on **insurance** and the Bed & Breakfast business.

Regardless of whether your business is in your home, on your property, around the corner, leased by you or a variation on these themes, insurance is one of the most important considerations you will have when running your Bed & Breakfast. It has the potential to protect your home and lifestyle in a way nothing else can – against the unexpected! After all, who can be properly prepared for the unexpected?

Insurance is a very simple concept. For an annual payment an insurance company agrees to provide specific cover for your **building and contents** and other B&B specific areas, including guests.

It should also have **business and liability cover**, which also may include activities you have for your guests.

Even if you believe you have adequate funds to replace or repair any loss that could occur, consideration must be given to investing in an insurance policy. In fact, in our increasingly litigious and varied society it would be irresponsible not to be adequately insured. Remember as a host, you have a responsibility not only to yourself and your family, but also to your guests.

So what constitutes adequate insurance in your specific case? Remembering that B&Bs are all different from each other, let us identify and evaluate the major areas of risk.

The biggest risk may in fact be the general public themselves. You have people coming to your home or property you do not know and who do not know you. You can never guess how they look after their own possessions, so how can you know how they will look after yours? Most B&B guests are the loveliest of people and some become life-long friends. Some, however, you will never please and you will wonder why they came in the first place. Things get broken perhaps, but no one confesses. Perhaps your lovely guest robes disappear after the guests leave. How do you handle situations like this and remain hospitable and content?

There are tricks of the trade concerning small losses and other operators will share some of these with you. Although your insurance policy should allow for claims of this nature, you may be penalised for continually making small claims. You need to realise that insurance companies are businesses as well.

An insurer has the right to decline to renew a policy, or even quote in the first instance, if they feel you are a bad risk, for example, if you make a lot of little claims on a continual basis.

Only you alone know your property intimately. Guests do not. In the dark, or in a strange place, people can get hurt. They don't know the stairs are a little uneven, or the coffee table is close to the sofa because the room is narrow. Perhaps they slip on a rug on the polished wooden floor, or in the night run into a piece of furniture or fall down the stairs.

You will need to look at your property through the eyes of a stranger and try to determine any potential risks. This is called risk management.

You can transfer these risks by taking out appropriate insurance coverage. The word 'appropriate' is important as many B&Bs pay for insurance each year, but don't have the cover they thought they had. Even worse, some do not have cover at all.

How can this be? Well, the first single most important thing to remember is that in most cases your current householders policy *will not cover you*. Be aware that many insurers do not insure B&Bs at all. This is not the negative it implies. If an insurance company doesn't understand what it is insuring, it is highly unlikely it will provide you with the type of policy you will require. If in doubt, ask questions!

One of the most important conditions of any policy is the duty of disclosure. For instance, your 'duty' would be to inform your current insurer once you decide to have paying guests or run a business from your home. This would also extend to long- or short-term paying students and to your staff.

You have an obligation to advise your insurance company of this and of any alterations you make to your home. Advising an insurance company in writing about the change from homeowner to B&B owner is imperative. It provides your insurers with accurate information and obliges them to confirm or decline your existing policy. Doing this in writing also provides some protection. You have a copy with details of when and to whom it was sent; secondly, written correspondence generally provokes a written response. This helps to protect you and substantiates basic information in the event of a dispute.

When writing to insurers be clear and specific and ask them for written confirmation for all areas of your cover, checking that you still have the elements needed from your domestic policy if you had one. Ask your local authority about insurance requirements.

You will need to advise your insurer:

◆ The number of guests you have facilities for.

◆ What specific changes you might make to your home, for example, renovations.

◆ Whether you have a restaurant, plan to serve morning or afternoon teas to guests or to the general public.

◆ Whether you will be serving or providing alcohol and any licences you may have that permit this.

◆ Whether you run any other business from your home or property. Many householders' policies exclude the running of any business from their home, and whether you employ staff, perhaps a gardener or casual cleaning person. If you are a B&B and pay people to work for you, you are no longer a domestic situation and your domestic policy, if you have one, will not cover you.

◆ Does your council have guidelines? Do you fall within these guidelines?

◆ What sort of activities do you provide for your guests? Are you on a farm and are the guests interacting with farm animals or perhaps farm life?

Many insurers neither understand nor wish to insure B&B accommodation and will tell you that quite clearly. Some may offer separate liability policies. That may solve one aspect of your insurance needs, but what does it mean for your building and contents cover?

Perhaps they offer to cover your home under a combined domestic and business policy. This can leave building and contents with very different, and usually less, cover than the cover you have enjoyed under a householder's policy.

This combined type of insurance cover requires you to pick and choose each section of cover, for example, glass, money, burglary and then to pay for basic covers automatically included in a B&B programme and householder's policy. Buying separate liability policies is expensive and can mean you have two or three different insurance companies covering your needs. If something happens, are these providers easily able to work together or will there be problems determining who is responsible for what because of the mishmash of policies put together like a patchwork quilt?

There are specific B&B programmes available. Don't rely on your current insurance intermediary to find one for you. Ask other operators for a referral or ask your local B&B association if there is one. They will usually be quite happy to help by passing on this information.

What must my B&B policy include as a minimum?
Your B&B policy must, without exception, cover you for buildings, guest house risks, business interruption, employer's liability, public liability, glass, money, and personal accident. Guest house risks will cover such areas as total contents, personal possessions, third party personal accident, guest's effects, frozen food, accidental loss of oil or metered water, replacement of external door locks and theft of garden furniture, and personal accident, which will cover assaults.

If you have a farm and already have one or other of these policies, do not assume it extends to your B&B as well. It probably won't, unless you have specifically arranged for it to do so.

Public liability relates to the general public in a business sense. It relates to injury and property damage caused by your personal negligence and/or business negligence. If part of your property is not well maintained and clear of debris, a guest may fall and sustain an injury. They may be able to claim compensation.

Product liability is in relation to any products you provide, but especially relevant to the food you serve. It doesn't matter whether you bought it from the bakery or not, should a guest find something 'extra' in it you are liable.

Manager liability may also be a consideration if you have staff looking after guests in your absence. Make certain they are covered in the event of a liability claim. You can be sure that if a guest decides to sue for negligence they will sue not only you and your business, but the staff or person representing you at the time.

Your B&B policy must, without exception, include fire, storm and tempest, burglary, malicious damage, fusion, glass and other covers, which your previous householder's policy had. It must cover your building and contents for the business of Bed & Breakfast, for housing guests (as many as you have facilities for), and their belongings. Your insurer must not be able to come back to you when you want to claim a broken window or a cracked hand basin and say, 'prove to us a guest did or didn't do it!'

There are very few insurance companies who provide a specific B&B policy. Those who do, generally provide this through an insurance intermediary. In the main, you will find this specialised cover is available as a specific scheme managed by that intermediary. Often it is less expensive to buy as direct as possible from those who manage and oversee the programme. The best place to find out about these people is through a referral from a B&B or from one of the B&B associations. These insurers will still have differences between the cover they offer and their service and involvement in the industry, but it will be specific to the B&B industry. Don't be afraid to get different quotes and ask as many questions as you can. This allows you to make educated decisions and buy as directly as possible.

What additional cover should I consider?

Business interruption is cover which replaces lost income in the event of a claim where your business is 'interrupted'. Generally, figures are based on your yearly income from the B&B. This is broken down into a weekly figure and about 70% of that income is insurable. In the event of a claim, a number of your expenses would stop, so the theory is 70% continue and roughly 30% stop. This can vary depending on your business. You also choose a term for this cover, for example, the number of weeks it would take to rebuild your property (always expect the worst case scenario) allowing for your location and perhaps construction, employing architects, etc.

This type of policy comes into play when there is physical damage to your property, and replaces income lost because you are unable to have guests.

It should guarantee to pay you on a weekly basis, not once the total claim amount is known, usually some months after the event. If you rely upon the income from your B&B to live, you simply must give careful consideration to this cover. Do you have an alternative source of income? How long could you survive without any income? Remember the bills don't stop because your income does.

You should be covered until you have regained the income you would normally expect, based on last year's figures, for that time of year. Even when the work to repair or replace is complete, it should pay on a descending scale until your business returns to normal, making up the difference allowing for the period you have chosen to cover.

Your building and contents insurance should reflect true replacement values. If you have more than one building it is advisable you show each building and the contents of each separately. Insurance is not based on a market value or saleable value. It is based on replacing or repairing. Therefore if you are unsure it is wise to ask a builder or valuer to provide you with an estimate based on your property. Add to that a percentage or lump sum allowance for removal of debris, architect's fees, council requirements, etc.

Allow a minimum of £3,000 or €4,700 as a rule of thumb. Many policies require you to insure for 80% of the actual replacement value. Therefore you need to know what those values are to insure them adequately. Any insurance policy is a legal, binding contract with terms and conditions.

If you provide activities for guests, you need to have them noted specifically on your policy and ensure when quoting, the intermediary understands what they are and how they are carried out. You know your place best. You know what things are available for guests and you may need to consider what, if any, are not to be made available to guests. Think long and hard about the risks involved with the activities you wish to offer.

Motor vehicles should be insured according to your insurer's criteria. Let them advise you how their policy works and how, what you are doing, will be interpreted by them. Some may allow you, as the directors of your business, to have a special notation rather than requiring you to insure for business use.

However, others may require you to insure for business use, usually at an increased cost. This would allow a claim under your tax. If you are thinking of picking up and dropping off guests check how this will affect your comprehensive motor policy and also your third party policy. You may have to change your third party insurance to a different code and generally at an increased cost. You should discuss your plans with your local motor insurer.

If you have enjoyed **personal accident and sickness/income protection** whilst in a position outside of the B&B, please keep it going. As we get older, it becomes more difficult to obtain this type of insurance. Once again, specialists in B&B insurance will know what options they have available for you.

Once you know you are going to employ staff, be they full time, part time or casual cleaners, chefs or gardeners, talk with the insurers in detail about **workers' compensation**. Your insurance intermediary can provide contact details.

Be aware that you should discuss with your builder any requirements for covering work carried out, should you need to repair or renovate. The best way to protect yourself in this respect is to employ a well known builder with a good reputation. He should carry his own insurance and be happy to show evidence of this to you.

Don't be afraid to ask questions about your existing insurance, or quotes that you obtain. Let the experts do what they do best and let them know what sorts of things concern you and just exactly what things you want to cover.

Find out about your insurance. It's best not to guess.

What you choose to insure, with whom, and to what value is up to you. Make informed decisions, ask questions, be involved in putting together your insurance policy.

Take your time and get it right. Remember that it is a small price to pay if something bad does happen and you will sleep as soundly as your guests – free of worry and confident in your insurance intermediary and your insurance policy, if you have taken the time to do it right.

PAYMENT

There is no set way of handling this part of your interaction with your guests. Some B&Bs prefer to settle the account at the beginning of the stay, particularly if you do not have extras that the guest can choose during their stay, while others keep to the traditional way of paying at the end. It is your establishment – the way you run it is up to you.

Either way, you will need to present your guest with an **itemised account**, retaining a duplicate yourself. This could be in the form of a handwritten invoice, which you can buy from your local stationers, or a computer generated account on your letterhead where you can store your record on disk.

METHODS OF PAYMENT

There are many different options for payment and you will need to decide which you will choose to accept. You might like to discuss your options and the positives and negatives of each with your financial adviser and bank manager. It is a good idea to list your payment options on your promotional literature.

Cash

This is the best option for any business because of the cleared funds aspect to **cash**. The only negatives are that you may be charged a small deposit fee and you will need a safe to store the money until you can go to the bank.

Cheques

Many establishments choose not to accept **cheques**, however, many of your guests will expect this facility. When accepting cheques, be sure to view the guest's cheque guarantee card or driver's licence and record the guest's details on the reverse side of the cheque. Ensure any alterations are initialled and the cheque is not post-dated. With the spread of cash machines it is reasonable to assume that cash or credit card usage will be the favoured method of payment.

Credit and debit cards

The financial size of your establishment will probably make the difference as to whether or not you choose to accept **credit** or **debit** cards. Many of your guests will want to settle their account by this method for it's the payment revolution of the 21st century. We use it to access our accounts to pay for petrol, groceries, pharmaceuticals, in fact almost everything you can think of. If you choose to go down this route there are a few things you will need to do. You need to apply for merchant card status from your bank. For the privilege of using their service you will pay a commission of around 2% of the face value of the payment. You will be given a floor limit, which usually equates to the charge of your cheapest night. Any charge after that will require an authorisation number. When applying for merchant card status be sure to have a telephone facility. This will allow you to take a non-refundable deposit. The hardware required is multifunctional in that it accepts both credit and debit card transactions. It works off modem-based technology. The set up costs, excluding the multi functional hardware, could be quite expensive, but is worthwhile if your property is a large guesthouse. Talk to your bank manager to ascertain the costs.

Traveller's cheques

Overseas guests are the most likely to use this form of 'currency' instead of credit or debit cards. If in English pounds or Euros they are as good as cash, but **travellers cheques** in foreign currency will require you to convert and to add the conversion service fee the bank will charge you. This can be quite problematic because your bank must be comfortable accepting and negotiating third party cheques, and this could be costly. Again, discuss this type of payment with your bank manager first. You will need to ensure the traveller produces suitable identification, eg a passport, and signs the cheque in front of you.

Foreign currency

If you choose to accept this you will need to convert the **foreign currency** into your country's currency and add the service fee the bank will charge you. Be aware that banks factor in a 4–5% margin, plus a fee for accepting and converting foreign currency. You must ensure you get the exchange rate from your bank. Get the money to the bank that day otherwise you may lose money on the transaction if the exchange rate changes. Try to encourage your guests to change the money themselves.

Pre-paid vouchers

One form of payment, which you may have to think about, is the **pre-paid voucher**. Many tour operators and other agencies issue these to their clients who then hand them to their B&B host in exchange for a night's stay. The accommodation may be pre-booked for an additional fee, or on a go-as-you please basis.

This arrangement has to be formally agreed to months in advance. The B&B host normally posts the voucher to a local agency, acting on behalf of the company which issued them. Systems can vary from company to company and there are usually additional agreements about supplements for extras of one kind or another, such as children sharing or 'superior accommodation', which must be paid directly to the host by the guest on the spot.

You may be approached individually about this type of business or it could be one of the many options open to you as a member of a consortium or B&B association. Either way you should discuss it fully with others already in the system before committing yourself. There is normally no cost involved for those agreeing to participate in voucher transactions. However, there may be a commission payable at some stage in the process. Check your voucher issuer for their procedure.

Travel agents are encouraging clients to purchase pre-paid accommodation vouchers before they leave home. This has resulted in an increase in the use of vouchers. The B&B voucher business is big and growing, especially where the Bed and Breakfast hosts are well organised and belong to their own associations. This is particularly the case throughout Ireland where a truly vast B&B voucher business has been painstakingly built up and finely tuned over the past 30 years or so.

The flexibility of B&B voucher programmes is very appealing to international visitors travelling around the UK and Ireland. Discover Travel & Tours is very well known within the international travel trade and is always looking for quality B&Bs, Inns and Guesthouses to join their programme – see their contact details under the 'Pre-Paid Voucher' heading in the Useful Addresses section.

FINANCIAL RECORDS

You need to keep records of your Bed & Breakfast's financial performance primarily for **taxation** purposes, but also to help monitor your business's growth. **VAT records** are required to be kept by all VAT-registered business operators. As we have said many times in this publication, it would be wise to contact a financial adviser prior to deciding anything to do with your Bed and Breakfast. The Inland Revenue office particularly, is a fount of information. You are legally required to keep your records for taxation purposes and the Inland Revenue has a CD-ROM designed for this purpose.

Sage, or a similar computer record-keeping program, is another worthwhile investment for record keeping and for tracking your business activities. Due to the complexities of tax systems, we will not be going into great depth about the records the government requires you to keep.

Other than recommending that you contact the Inland Revenue we would suggest you apply to your nearest VAT office for registration if required. Customs and Excise administer this office. A VAT registered business must show its nine-digit VAT number on all literature and documentation pertaining to the business.

As for the figures you need to assess your financial progress, we would suggest that every month you reconcile and look at the following.

Accommodation cash flow

This is the permanent record of your occupancy and income. With this information you can compare month-to-month, year-to-year trading, highlighting regular seasonal highs and lows and allowing you to forecast accurately. You can then turn this information into graphs, perhaps even comparing weekend and weekday trade, to plan for the coming year or season. As months go by you will be able to make decisions on when your busiest periods are, enabling you to market to fill in the gaps or even the best time for you to take a well-earned break.

Operating expenses

These are the fixed costs each month such as: leases, rent, rates, insurance, loans, memberships, etc; plus your variable costs such as: telephone, electricity, gas, water, labour (including your own), food, decoration, etc. Again, graphs are a great tool for comparison and can help determine whether further investigation is needed.

For example one month you may have spent £300 or €250 on food, while the next you only spent £210 or €180, but your accommodation receipts were similar. Ask yourself what changed.

Break-even analysis

The combination of your operating expenses and your accommodation cash flow provides you with the material to prepare a **break-even analysis**. When your costs are higher than your income you are running at a loss. Break-even is the point when the two meet, and all income above that is profit.

Bank balances

Another long-term indicator is the comparison between your opening and closing **bank balance** each month. It helps track your expenditure and is also good to convert to graph form.

Debtors and creditors

Monthly reconciliation of the money owed to you by **debtors**, and by you to **creditors**, is imperative when running a successful business. Ensure that you pay by your due date, as you want to maintain a good credit rating, particularly if you are part of a small community. You should ensure you put in place a process to follow up debtors. While they are not paying you, you are losing valuable interest.

Profit and loss statement

This is the conclusion of all of the above. Subtracting your costs from actual sales revenue from accommodation receipts will give you a gross profit estimate for the month. Then subtract all other costs including a pro rata amount for variable expenditure. This will give you a net profit figure.

The **net profit** is the bottom line figure from which you can draw cash, pay off capital or retain cash in the business for future growth. It is also the figure you can match against the value of your business assets to see the return on your investments.

With all these figures at your fingertips you can build an accurate picture of the financial position of your business. Recording these figures each month gives you the ability to keep your business finely tuned. You will be able to see trends in profits, costs and sales. It will also help you to see any potential problems if one or more of these indicators begin to go off track.

A business will eventually fail if it is not profitable. It may also fail even if it is profitable on paper, but when cash flow is not monitored to ensure that debts are paid when due or you take too much cash out of the business.

General ledger

A **general ledger** is a day-by-day record of your daily incomings and outgoings. In any business, including B&Bs, you need to ensure a general ledger is established and maintained in order to monitor debits and credits against each salient item. An accountant or financial adviser is the best person to assist you in setting up your books, in particular your general ledger. Again, a suitable commercial program can help you.

BANKING

It is imperative that you put your payments into the bank as quickly as possible, for both security and financial reasons.

If you are unable to get to your bank every day, and have the potential to carry large sums of money on your premises, you must inform your insurance company. We would also suggest the installation of a small safe.

A meeting with your bank manager would be a good idea when starting up your business. Your bank should be able to advise you of the best accounts to run your business and will provide you with the necessary documentation that will need to accompany any transaction.

To make your time at the bank more efficient:

◆ Always sort coins and notes into denominations and place like coins in the bags provided by the bank.

◆ List your cheques on the deposit slip.

◆ Pay your foreign currency to the bank using a separate slip.

◆ Don't forget that for credit card transactions there is nothing to bank as the payments are electronic. Debit card transactions are made straight into your account.

If you are unable to get to the bank during trading hours, find out if the bank has a **night safe facility**. The bank will be able to issue you with a commercial wallet in which to put your money. The bank will also give you a key or a code that will unlock the night safe.

8

Housekeeping

Housekeeping is the centrepiece of successful Bed & Breakfast operation. Any B&B owner will tell you that *if you are not fond of housekeeping, and if you are not particularly good at it, then Bed and Breakfast is not for you.*

Look around your house. Are you one of those people where everything has a place? Do you regularly clean under the beds? Do you lift all your ornaments up and individually wipe them and the surface beneath them every time you clean? Do you clean around plugholes with a toothbrush? Does your house have the air of a magazine layout?

You do and it does? Good! You are exactly the sort of person who should run a Bed & Breakfast. You can never be too clean when operating a B&B. Cleanliness that is good enough for friends and family may not be good enough for paying guests. The two things that will destroy your reputation as a host are bad beds, and therefore a bad night's sleep, and a 'dirty' house.

Remember that your idea of a clean house may not be the same as your guests. Think of Felix Unger in *The Odd Couple*, he was the

neat freak. Now multiply him tenfold. That is
the standard you need to reach. Even though
your guests have chosen Bed and Breakfast for
its 'homely' atmosphere, what they actually
want is the picture book version of home.

TIP

If you don't like cleaning or
ironing don't get into this
business!

They want everything to be spotlessly clean and sparkling. They
don't want to be reminded of the hundreds of guests who have
stayed in the room before them. They want to feel that the room is
as new. Immaculate cleanliness is the best way to achieve this and it
will win you brownie points in the word of mouth stakes.

BEING PREPARED

When getting ready to clean ensure that you are suitably attired.
Wear flat, rubber soled shoes and gloves. Be very careful when
emptying rubbish bins, as you do not know what people may leave
behind.

Having a cupboard in your laundry designated for cleaning
products is a good idea. Ensure that you know what chemicals are
in each product and the treatment in event of accidental poisoning.

A CLEANING CHECKLIST

We would suggest that you create a **checklist**
for cleaning each room. This will serve as a
reminder that you have covered everything
when setting up for your guest, and as a guide
for any outside help. The list below can be
used as a guide, but you may need to add
items based on your facilities.

TIP

When cleaning watch for small
details as the big things always
get done.

Bathrooms

◆ Use disinfectant to clean the toilet bowl, inside and out.

◆ Mop the floor.

◆ Polish glass and mirrors.

◆ Scrub the bath and shower. If you have a spa bath or jacuzzi clean it thoroughly using recommended products. These facilities can be a hotbed for germs, particularly jacuzzis, if you don't take special care.

◆ Unclog any drains.

◆ Empty rubbish bins.

◆ Disinfect all surfaces.

◆ Throw out any used soap, shampoo and conditioner.

◆ Wipe down any ornaments and decorative items.

> **TIP**
>
> Providing toiletries enhances the feeling of indulgence and can be a welcome relief to forgetful guests.

◆ Wipe down all drawers, inside and out.

◆ Wipe down blinds and windowsills.

◆ Wipe shower curtains daily and machine wash them regularly to prevent mould.

◆ Remove any used towels, robes, etc.

◆ Restock toilet paper.

◆ Replace towels, hand towels and bath mats with clean ones, including spares.

◆ Replace robes with clean ones.

◆ Replace any toiletries you provide.

> **TIP**
>
> White towels absorb water better than coloured ones and can be bleached.

◆ Fill up the soap dispenser near the washbasin.

◆ Check that all the lights are working.

◆ Wipe down all tiles.

Bedrooms

◆ Dust and polish all surfaces.

◆ Wipe down all ornaments.

◆ Polish glass and mirrors.

◆ Strip beds and replace sheets and pillowcases.

◆ Air blankets, pillows, blankets and continental quilts regularly.

◆ Sweep, vacuum and mop floors as appropriate, including under beds and furniture.

> **TIP**
>
> Provide two pillows and two towels per person.
> White linen is recommended as it does not fade, can be bleached and always matches.

◆ Check that all light bulbs are working.

◆ Empty all rubbish bins.

◆ Put everything back in place.

◆ Check drawers for anything left behind. Anything left by guests should be removed. Phone them and post it back.

◆ Wipe down windowsills and clean windows.

◆ Air the room by leaving windows open for at least an hour after every guest has left.

◆ Wipe down skirting boards and picture rails.

> **TIP**
>
> Guests should be able to read comfortably in bed.

+ Wipe down furniture.

+ Check for any marks or scuffs on walls.

+ Replace any used glasses or cups with clean ones.

+ Replace any used coffee or tea.

+ Replace any brochures, literature, discount coupons, etc.

+ Use air freshener or light an aromatic candle.

Common rooms

+ Dust and polish all surfaces.

+ Wipe down all ornaments.

+ Polish glass and mirrors.

+ Sweep, vacuum and mop floors as appropriate, including under furniture.

+ Vacuum under chair cushions.

+ Wipe down furniture.

+ Check all light bulbs are working.

+ Empty all rubbish bins.

+ Put everything back in place.

+ Wipe down windowsills and clean windows.

+ Wipe down skirting boards and picture rails.

- Check for any marks or scuffs on walls.

- Replace any brochures, literature, discount coupons, etc.

- Air the room as much as possible when there are no guests.

- Wipe down door handles.

- Wipe down telephone handsets.

- If you allow smoking in any of your common rooms ensure that you empty and rinse out ashtrays several times a day. Cigarette smoke is invasive and will impregnate all your soft furnishings.

- Always leave a window open in this room to allow some of the smoke to escape.

- Use air freshener or light an aromatic candle.

> **TIP**
>
> Newspaper and water cleans glass quickly and effectively.

Kitchen

- Wipe down windowsills and clean windows.

- Wipe down skirting boards and picture rails.

- Check for any marks or scuffs on walls.

- Empty all rubbish bins at least daily.

- Sweep and mop floors at least daily or more frequently as required.

- Keep all surfaces clean from dust, food scraps and grease.

- Wash tea towels daily.

- Keep cloths clean and disinfected.

> **TIP**
>
> Cloths: use different colours for different purposes, one for the floor, one for washing up, one for wiping vegetable chopping boards, one for wiping meat chopping boards, etc.

TIP

Don't forget to have a fire extinguisher and a fire blanket in the kitchen.

◆ Use the dishwasher where possible.

◆ Clean the oven regularly.

◆ Wipe down the fridge regularly.

◆ Wipe out cupboards and pantry weekly.

◆ Check that all light and power points are functioning.

TAKING CARE OF YOUR FURNITURE

You need to remember that your **furniture** has now also become the property of your guests. They, however, may not take as good care of it as you would. Thus, it becomes your responsibility to take care of it enough for all of you. Following are some hints to help you do this.

◆ Take care to handle your furniture carefully. Bumps will mar wooden furniture. When you need to vacuum or mop the floors, it is better to move the furniture.

◆ Any spills should be wiped up immediately.

◆ Provide plenty of coasters on coffee tables, bedside tables, lamp tables, etc. and encourage guests to use them.

◆ Wipe furniture daily.

◆ Have your couches professionally cleaned regularly.

TIP

Sticky marks on furniture can be removed by one tablespoon of vinegar to one litre of water.

◆ A good cleaning fluid does wonders on most surfaces, including granite.

◆ Put adhesive felt on the bottom of ornaments to protect the surface of your furniture.

THE OUTSIDE

While cleaning the inside is important, ensure you don't forget the outside of your house. Any marks on your house façade should be fixed before they are a problem.

- Sweep paths to the house daily.

- Wipe down the outside of your door.

- Polish your letterbox, door handle, knocker and bell.

- Sweep and mop the entrance areas.

- Keep the windows clean.

- Wipe down outdoor furniture daily, so guests feel they can use it.

- Wipe down any tables after use.

- Mow lawns regularly.

- Keep paths free from weeds and overgrown plants and remove and replace plants as need dictates. Gardens need to be tended and your guests will appreciate the care you take of their sanctuary (and yours)!

- Check outdoor lighting nightly to ensure the bulbs are functioning.

- Check roof tiles regularly. A loose tile can cause havoc inside and out.

TIP
Check around the house for cobwebs each day and remove them straight away.

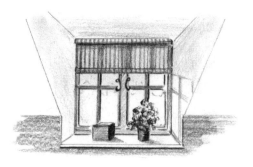

9

Occupational Health & Safety

I t is your duty to yourself, your family, your employees and your guests to provide a safe place in which to live, work and stay. To help facilitate this we suggest you set down a few guidelines that will cover fire safety, work practices and general instructions for guests.

FIRE SAFETY

The first step is to contact your local fire department and ask them to visit your B&B to identify potential hazards.

Follow your local fire authority instructions to the letter and have them train you, your family and your staff on the use of your fire blanket and fire extinguisher which you are required to provide in the kitchen and common areas. Recommendations will involve such procedures as smoke alarms in every guest bedroom, in your own bedrooms, outside your kitchen and in hallways. Having a heritage listed home may give you a bit of leeway in the placement of alarms. You cannot legally, or morally for that matter, operate a Bed & Breakfast without smoke alarms.

◆ Go around your house and replace any double adaptors with power boards. Double adaptors are one of the main causes of domestic fires.

- Your insurance policy may also stipulate certain requirements as part of your insurance cover. Ensure that you adhere to any requirement.

- As guests check in draw their attention to exits and the storage places for fire blankets and fire extinguishers. Advise your guests of a common meeting place outside the property in the event of a fire.

- Leave your reservation diary near the door at night so you can easily check everyone off and ensure that everyone is safe.

- Never deadlock your door while you or guests are inside. In the event of a fire you may not be able to escape.

A SAFE PLACE TO STAY

Room by room you need to establish that your house is as safe as it can possibly be.

In the **bathrooms** you need to ensure bathmats have non-slip backing, that the room is thoroughly disinfected after each guest's visit, that guests do not share bar soap and that no medication is kept in the bathroom. You might want to consider installing handrails near the bath and the shower.

The **kitchen** can be a hotbed for germs. You need to keep pets out of the kitchen and any dining areas. Any detergents and cleaning agents should be kept in a cupboard separate from food. Ensure you know how to treat poisoning that can occur from oral or eye contact of any of these agents. You should neither smoke nor eat when preparing food. Use separate cutting boards for meat and vegetables – label them accordingly. Keep fridge temperatures at 5° Celsius. Cover any wounds with band-aids and gloves. Ensure you reheat foods thoroughly. Cover food prior to serving. Wear gloves when preparing food as much as practicable. These aspects will be covered in your certificate of compliance.

In **common areas** you should ensure lighting is adequate, and that smoke detectors are installed in all guest bedrooms, hallways and common areas. Ensure that all stairs have handrails. Electrical wiring should be inspected regularly. Think about installing safety switches to protect you from power surges. Ensure rugs are taped down or have a non-slip backing. If you are planning on accommodating families, particularly toddlers, you might want to consider safety plugs for power points, safety latches on low cabinets and gates for stairs. Leave emergency numbers by the phone.

Outside you should ensure your property is well lit, that paving is in good repair and that any steps are not slippery.

A SAFE PLACE TO WORK

Not only should your Bed & Breakfast be a safe place to stay, you need to ensure it is a safe place to work.

Train your staff and your family on fire procedures and how to use extinguishers and fire blankets. Have quarterly fire drills to ensure everyone knows the location of the outside meeting point.

Another safety precaution would be Hepatitis B vaccinations. Hepatitis is a rapidly spreading disease in all its permutations. As you are handling both food and cleaning it might be a good investment to have a vaccination. See your local doctor.

Wear clean clothes and rubber based shoes when cleaning, as you don't want to spread germs. The most important thing you can wear when you clean, however, is a pair of gloves. It will protect you from all of the bacteria that you will encounter. Use different gloves for cleaning bathrooms from those you wear for cleaning any other room in the house. Do not touch your face with these gloves.

Safety in the kitchen

Safety in the kitchen is two-fold. It is about protecting you from accidents, in the most accident-prone place in your house, and protecting you and your guests from diseases, the obvious one being food poisoning.

In certain areas, you must undertake **food-handling courses** at your nearest accredited learning facility. If it is not compulsory in your area, we would recommend you consider taking one of the recognised courses. They are normally only one or two days and can save you and your business a lot of anguish in the long run. They will teach you about effective hygiene practices, food storage, cleaning and sanitising, avoiding food contamination, food legislation and understanding legal obligations.

There are a number of things you can do that will minimise accidents in your kitchen.

- Don't rush around the kitchen. Working methodically is more productive in the long run and minimises any chance of slipping.

- Keep knives sharp and clean. Never wash them in soapy water with other items – someone is likely to cut him or herself. When sharpening knives do it away from your body. When wiping them do so with the sharp end pointed away from you. Always use the correct knife for the job.

◆ Your clothing should offer protection. Long sleeves will protect your arms from steam, and aprons will protect your body and clothes from the stove.

◆ Use a dry cloth or oven mitt when handling hot dinner plates and saucepans. A damp cloth will heat up, create steam, and ultimately result in a scald.

◆ Saucepan handles should not protrude over the edge of the stove as it can create accidents. Use both hands, protected with mitts, to carry saucepans.

◆ Arrange your oven shelves before you turn the oven on. This will help prevent burns.

◆ Mop any spills immediately to prevent slipping.

THE FUTURE

While absolute food safety cannot be guaranteed by regulations, it is possible to minimise the risk to public health by introducing measures leading to improvements in hygienic production and handling of food, in direct response to the proposed hazard posed. Contact your local Health Authority for requirements.

It is important to appreciate the significant costs attributable to food-borne disease (entire loss of business) and the savings that could be achieved as a result of the reform of food hygiene regulations. By reducing the incidence of food-borne illness, the proposed, risk-based, preventative food hygiene standards will have specific benefits for many sectors of the community including:

- **Consumers**: through fewer incidents of food-borne illness and lower associated medical costs.

- **The domestic food industry**: through increased consumer confidence and a move to less prescriptive and nationally uniform outcome-based regulations.

- **Employers**, in both the private and public sectors: as less sick-leave would be taken due to the reduced influence of food-borne illness.

- **Other industry sectors**: such as tourism, which will benefit through increased customer confidence.

Identify the hazards: Some hazards can be controlled, while others may be beyond our control. For example the quality of raw materials you receive is the responsibility of your suppliers.

Identify the critical control points: These are the points at which important processes can go wrong.

The difference between a critical control point (CCP) and a hazard is that a CCP can be controlled and monitored. Temperature control in chillers and cold-rooms is a good example of a CCP.

> **TIP**
>
> Wash all fruit and vegetables to remove soil, bacteria, insects and chemicals.

Set the critical limits for each CCP
If you exceed these limits you could face a major problem – for example if your cool-room were running at a temperature of 10°C, this would be a problem.

Monitor the CCPs: Every CCP will require monitoring to make sure you do not exceed the critical limit. In the cool-room you would need to monitor the temperature using a hand-held thermometer.

Establish corrective action: Decide what action is to be taken if the critical limits are exceeded. If your cool-room is too warm you should adjust the temperature or call the technician.

Set up records

This is one of the most important steps because records can prove your compliance. Records are also useful in training your staff and tracking results, for example, regularly recording the cool-room temperature on a chart.

Will my business have to comply?

Businesses, which provide, produce, or package food for consumption by the general public are required to comply with all existing legislation.

FIRST AID

You have a moral, if not legal, obligation to be able to provide **first aid** to your staff and guests. One member of your staff or family being qualified is probably enough, but it should be the person who is primarily running the establishment. Everyone in the household should know and understand your establishment's procedures for handling an emergency.

One thing you must do is purchase a comprehensive first aid kit. You need to maintain this kit and log any incidents that occur. You can purchase this on the web from St John Ambulance (www.sja.ork.uk/).

10

Food and the Bed & Breakfast

We now reach the breakfast part of the Bed & Breakfast. Your house is ready, your marketing and business plans are in place, and your guests are on their way. What are you going to do about breakfast?

BREAKFAST OPTIONS

The fully cooked breakfast

This is your opportunity to shine. By now your guests should have had a sample of your cooking with afternoon tea on the day of their arrival. However, breakfast is the meal your guests have been waiting for. Most guests will be looking forward to the Great British, Scottish, Welsh, Ulster or Irish Fry-up, that is, the famous **cooked breakfast** that is still so popular with many people on holiday.

Start with the basics: a few cereals, fresh fruit juice, fruit compote or fruit, freshly baked bread, conserves, speciality teas and brewed coffee. Muffins and croissants are a nice extra.

Your guests may not want all the above, but it should be on offer. What most will want is a hot meal and something different from what they would prepare at home. Our suggestion is that you offer a few different options for the guest to choose from.

The trick here is to be imaginative. Look in the hundreds of wonderful cookbooks that are released each year and experiment with them. Don't, however, experiment on your guests. If you want to try something new, try it on your friends and family first.

There are great recipes that have a twist on the traditional. For example, Eggs Benedict served on muffins with smoked salmon, French toast mixed with cinnamon sugar, and orange juice, savoury pancakes and crepes. You can run the gamut from the traditional to the experimental, but you should have fun with it.

You don't need to offer a huge variety every day. What is better is to have one or two special dishes available every day and to rotate them, so that guests who are staying more than one night have some variety. Having staples such as bacon, eggs, mushrooms and tomatoes in your cupboard will serve you well for those guests who prefer more traditional fare.

As for quantity you don't want to scrimp. Most guests won't be greedy, but they will want a hearty breakfast. The one disadvantage of having 'breakfast' in your type of accommodation is that some guests will feel they should be able to eat as much as possible. You will need to factor this into your room rate/tariff.

Presentation is almost as important as the food itself. When serving your breakfast you need to look at the aesthetic appearance of the food through the eyes of a paying guest. Take into account colour, texture and smell. The appreciation of food is through all five senses so you should ensure you consider all of them when serving your meal.

The continental breakfast

The **continental breakfast** traditionally consists of a croissant or Danish pastry with coffee or tea, and if you are lucky a glass of juice.

Some Bed & Breakfasts are offering continental breakfast, but are actually providing fruit, toast, tea and coffee. We do not believe either of these options is good enough if you want to gain recognition as a superior Bed & Breakfast. Most guests use the occasion of staying in a Bed & Breakfast as an opportunity to experience a cooked breakfast – if they wanted tea and toast they would have stayed at home. However the option of a simple breakfast with toast or a continental breakfast could be offered for those who desire a lighter meal.

The breakfast basket

The provision of a **breakfast basket** is popular with those guests who want to be out and about early, for example, walkers and cyclists. It can contain fresh juice, fresh fruit compotes with yoghurt, freshly baked bread with jams and conserves, butter, a thermos of tea or coffee and often freshly baked goods such as Danish pastries and muffins and the appropriate eating and drinking utensils. If there are cooking facilities you can also supply bacon, eggs, or freshly made speciality sausages.

Presentation is very important here. You won't have the opportunity to impress with your cooking, although the freshly baked goods will help, so you need to focus on how you are going to present your breakfast. Make your basket look like a gift to the guest. Linen

TIP

Make your breakfasts exciting, if guests stay for more than one night vary the menu so they have a selling point for you, when talking to others.

napkins, rolled in a decorative napkin ring, will add a special touch. Have a look in some cookbooks for ideas.

LUNCH

This is really up to you, and very few guests will expect it. If you do offer it, do so at an extra cost. Remember that preparing **lunch** for your guests will really break into your day. The amount you charge may never make up for the time you will have to spend preparing it.

A **picnic basket**, provided at an extra cost, is a popular option for the guests. This, as with the breakfast basket, is particularly popular in areas where people are likely to explore the natural wonders in the surrounding area. Preparation time is much the same as for an in-house lunch, but there is little cleaning up afterwards.

MORNING AND AFTERNOON TEA

As mentioned before it is a great idea to welcome your travel weary guests with **morning** or **afternoon tea**. The traditional version of this is tea or coffee with home-baked goodies, such as scones or pancakes.

Some B&Bs are experimenting here as well. They are welcoming their guests with cheese, dips and antipasto. The only drawback with this is it doesn't fill your house with the same aroma as freshly baked biscuits.

This is a great opportunity to catch up with your guests, find out their plans and give them some advice on your locality. You can use the opportunity to set down any house rules you might have and acquaint them with fire escapes, etc.

If you have a large establishment you could provide a high tea, with dainty sandwiches and cakes, scones, a selection of wonderful teas and coffees and even the occasional string quartet. In this way you could add some theatre to your establishment and earn some extra money, making it an open house.

DINNER

Some Bed & Breakfasts and Guesthouses offer a **weekend gourmet package**, which includes the evening meal for one or more nights. This is particularly useful if you don't have a variety of restaurants in your locality that you can happily recommend. Again, experiment with some of the wonderful cookbooks on the market and try to use as much local produce as possible. Any cookbook by local writers and cooks is a great place to start.

> **TIP**
>
> Always be prepared to make another pot of coffee and have refreshments freely available.

If your guest asks to stay in for dinner without much warning you need to do two things. Charge them, and let them know that they have to have what you happen to keep in stock, or they can have what you and your family are eating. The cost charged should reflect the meal you are serving.

If you are going to cook dinner be sure you purchase fresh meat from a quality butcher, fresh vegetables and fruit from a quality grocer and seafood from a specialist. Don't purchase these items from a supermarket, as the quality is not consistent. You want to be remembered as the host that provided a quality meal.

EATING WITH GUESTS

This is really up to you and your guests. Breakfast is quite a difficult meal to serve and eat at the same time. You will also find your guests will sleep in and you will need your strength for the day ahead. Of all international guests, Australians tend to be a bit shy at breakfast, we would suggest you let guests have this meal to themselves.

Some guests are frequently not very comfortable sharing breakfast tables with each other, tending to be a bit monosyllabic and uncommunicative. You might find it better to ensure you have a few separate tables where couples can have breakfast 'alone'. Ask them for their seating preference the evening before.

If you are serving dinner there is no reason why you should not eat with your guests. It is quite likely that if your guests have chosen to eat at home they would like some company. Don't overpower the conversation, but feel free to let your natural personality shine.

KNOWING THE RESTAURANTS AND PUBS IN YOUR AREA

You need to become an expert on the cafes, pubs and restaurants in your area.

This is one of the most important recommendations you will be asked to give. You need to have tried the restaurants you recommend as, like it or not, you will be judged on the quality of your recommendation.

By being part of your local tourism body you will meet many of the restaurateurs in your area. You may be able to arrange a 10% discount for your guests, or a free cup of coffee, or even a free meal for you and your partner for every 10 recommendations you send their way. Never enter into an arrangement such as this, however, unless you really believe the restaurant is up to scratch. A 'free' dinner for you is no reason to destroy your credibility. Your reputation is worth much more than that.

PRESENTATION

It is very important that you present your food to the best of your ability. Whilst I am passionate about increasing the professionalism of the industry I am equally passionate about Bed & Breakfasts retaining their individuality, or what makes them unique. If it is your style to provide sugar in a sugar bowl, then, as long as you provide a sugar spoon, feel free to do so in your B&B. The same applies to jams and conserves. This is your home and it is these small touches that your guests will be looking forward to during their stay.

ALCOHOL LICENCES

We asked two leading legal firms for their comments on the Alcohol Licensing Act as it applies to Bed & Breakfast and Guesthouse owners.

England and Wales

Matthew Welch, a partner at Fisher Jones Greenwood Solicitors, London, gave us the following advice on the type of alcohol licence a Bed & Breakfast owner could/should apply for, if your property is located in either England or Wales:

If you are running a guesthouse, you can either apply for a residential licence or a combined restaurant and residential licence.

The first step I advise you to take is to contact your local magistrates court and ask them for a copy of their local licensing policy. It may also be useful to speak to the licensing officer at the police station.

The residential licence will allow you to sell alcohol to residents of the bed and breakfast, but is subject to the condition that the alcohol shall not be sold or supplied other than to persons residing at the bed and breakfast or their private friends, who are bona fide, and entertained at the guest's expense.

It also covers consumption by the guest or the guest's friend, entertained by the guest, either on the premises or with a meal supplied at the guesthouse, but to be consumed off the premises. This means you can supply beer or wine with packed lunches.

The restaurant licence allows drink to be supplied as an ancillary to a table meal and would allow you therefore to supply drink to people using the restaurant who would not necessarily be guests at the bed and breakfast.

Please note that if you apply for a residential licence, the magistrates will almost undoubtedly make it a condition that you shall also provide on the premises for guests, adequate seating accommodation in a room not used for sleeping, serving meals or for the supply of drink. This is commonly called a dry room and can make obtaining a licence an expensive exercise, as you have to devote a single room to this purpose.

The magistrates court will tell you their scale of fees, but the court fees are normally quite reasonable and usually the fee for applying for a licence is £30. The magistrates court policy should set out the names and addresses of all the people to whom you should send notice of your application.

Ireland

Kenneth Morgan, at William Fry Solicitors, Dublin, gave us the following advice on the type of alcohol licence available for Bed &

Breakfast and Guesthouse operators in the Republic of Ireland:

The position in Ireland is governed by an Intoxicating Liquor Licensing code, which has application to all premises where alcohol is sold for consumption on or off the premises. A Licence is required in all circumstances for the retail sale of alcohol. The running of a Bed & Breakfast or a Guesthouse is governed by standards enforced by Bord Fáilte and the body known as Excellence in Tourism.

Where a B&B or Guesthouse wishes to sell wine, an application for a Wine Retailer's On-Licence must be made to the Collector of Customs & Excise. An application to Court is not required. The Collector will authorise an official to visit the premises to verify that the premises are suitable for a Wine Retailer's On-Licence. The process will take one month; upon the expiry of that period and in the absence of any objections the Licence will issue upon payment of the Excise Duty. In our experience the issue of such licences is relatively straightforward. The Licence remains in force until the end of the licensing year – 30 September – and then must be renewed for the subsequent twelve months.

Where the Wine Retailer's On-Licence attaches to a 'restaurant', beer may be sold for consumption on the premises provided that the beer is consumed at the same time with a meal and paid for at the same time as the meal is paid for; the restaurant is not entitled to a bar counter.

To qualify as a restaurant, one must hold a Restaurant Certificate. This can only be obtained from the local District Court and must receive the consent of the Garda Síochána. The local Superintendent, in whose area the premises are located, must be satisfied that the application is bona fide and he/she will be represented at the court hearing.

It is important to emphasise that a B&B or Guesthouse is not entitled to sell beer unless it attaches to a certified restaurant. Under no circumstances may spirits be sold on the premises unless the B&B or Guesthouse has been granted a Special Restaurant Licence or a full Publican's Licence.

Whilst it may be the practice that a glass of wine or bottle of beer is provided as part of a meal on an informal basis in a B&B or Guesthouse this amounts to a breach of the Licensing Code – unless offered gratuitously.

PURCHASING TIPS

The quality of your produce will be reflected in your meal. Your guests will expect as much **fresh produce**, preferably locally grown, as possible. One of the most important things you can do before even thinking of serving up a meal for your guests is to find suppliers for all of your food needs. Good suppliers for meat, fruit and vegetables, seafood and poultry are very important – as stated before, you will rarely find the quality you need at a supermarket.

A good baker is handy, but with the proliferation of bread makers on the market there is no reason that you can't bake your own. Be aware when purchasing a bread maker that many suppress the aroma. Be wary of purchasing one of these – you want the smell of freshly baked bread wafting through the house. Your guests will love it.

A delicatessen is another worthwhile find. You will be able to purchase some fantastic cheeses here, and many other great treats.

RECIPE IDEAS

Nectarines in Passionfruit Syrup
$^1/_3$ cup sugar
$^1/_2$ cup passionfruit pulp (fresh or tinned)
$2^1/_2$ cups water
8 white nectarines, halved and stones removed

Place sugar, passionfruit and water into a deep, heavy base saucepan over a medium heat, simmer for 5 minutes until slightly syrupy. Add more sugar, if necessary. Add nectarines and simmer for one minute on both sides or until just soft. Place nectarines in serving bowls, strain pips from passionfruit syrup, pour over nectarines. Serve warm or chilled. Serves 4.

Baked Peach Brioche
8 small slices of brioche or fruit bread
100 g of cream cheese
3 tblsp castor sugar
1 tsp vanilla extract
4 peaches, sliced
$^1/_3$ cup of icing sugar

Place the brioche slices in a baking dish lined with baking paper or foil. Combine the cream cheese, sugar and vanilla in a bowl and spread on the brioche. Top with peach slices and sprinkle heavily with icing sugar. Bake in a preheated oven at 200°C for 20 minutes or until the peaches are golden. Serve warm or cold.

Raspberry Puffs
1 cup self-raising flour
$^1/_2$ cup icing sugar
1 tsp baking power

2 eggs
60 g butter, melted
$^1/_2$ cup milk
300 g raspberries
Icing sugar and lemon wedges to serve

Place flour, icing sugar and baking powder in a bowl. Add eggs, butter and mix until smooth. Mix in raspberries. Drop spoonfuls of mixture into a non-stick fry pan over a medium heat and cook until the puffs are golden and puffed. To serve, sprinkle with icing sugar and a slice of lemon. Serves 4.

Salmon Puffs
Smoked salmon
2 leeks, cleaned and cut into rings, white part only

Filling
300 g ricotta cheese
300 g Gruyère cheese, grated
2 tblsps dill, chopped
2 tblsps capers, chopped

Mix filling together.

8 sheets Filo pastry
Brush every second sheet with soft butter
Poppy seeds

Layer in an ovenproof dish or in individual muffin tins: 2 sheets pastry, filling, leeks, one or two rings for the individual puffs, salmon. Top with 2 layers of pastry, brush with butter and sprinkle with poppy seeds. Bake 200°C, 40 minutes for the large pie, 20 minutes for the individual pies. Serves 6.

Mediterranean Omelette

1 red capsicum

6 slices prosciutto, roughly chopped

3 spring onions thinly sliced

40 g fetta cheese, crumbled

40 g Parmesan cheese, grated

4 free range eggs

150 ml milk

1 tsp olive oil

Cut capsicum into small flat pieces, place under a hot grill until skin blackens and blisters. Place in bowl. Cover tightly with plastic wrap, leave for 10 minutes then rub off skin and discard. Cut capsicum into thin strips. Heat olive oil in frying pan and sauté prosciutto until crisp. Whisk eggs and milk together, pour into oiled, ovenproof pan. Scatter capsicum, prosciutto and onions over eggs. Bake 180°C, for 30 minutes or until filling is just set. Serves 4–6.

Easy breakfast puff pie

$^1/_2$ cup chopped onion

$^1/_2$ cup chopped courgettes

2 ounces cooked ham steak, cubed

$1^1/_4$ ounces shredded cheddar cheese

2 tblsps sour cream

2 eggs (or 3 egg whites)

a pinch of pepper

Preheat oven to 350° Fahrenheit. Spray 9-inch pie plate with non-stick spray. Spray frying pan with non-stick spray; add onion, zucchini and ham. Cook about 2 minutes until translucent. Spread onion mixture over bottom of pie plate, add beaten eggs. Sprinkle cheese on top. Bake until golden brown and puffy (35 to 45 minutes.) Serves 4.

Be as flexible as possible when it comes to **breakfast serving times**. Some guests like to take the opportunity to get up early, while others like to sleep in. There is no harm, however, in asking an approximate time the evening before so you can plan your day, or in letting your guest know when you plan to finish serving breakfast.

Like everything you do in this most competitive of businesses, your breakfasts must be first class. If you serve ordinary white bread and jams in sachets, longlife milk and a variety of cereals in little cardboard packets, you can be sure that if your guests do come back it won't be for the breakfasts!

Even if you consider yourself the world's worst cook, with a little help and imagination you can still come up with a great breakfast. With bread machines and good quality flours available there's no excuse for serving the bland packaged breads that abound. You may have access to a really good bakery. If you do not, have a go at baking yourself. It's not too hard and your guests will appreciate the effort. The same goes for jams and marmalades. If you don't fancy trying to make your own, there's nearly always a little old lady nearby who makes wonderful preserves. A little research and effort on your part will pay dividends. And remember, there's nothing wrong with bacon and eggs. Even if it isn't new and trendy, it's for good reason that it's the singular most endurable breakfast dish in the western world! Just make sure the eggs are good and fresh and the bacon is top quality.

> **TIP**
>
> To check if an egg is fresh drop it gently in a glass of cold water. If it sinks it is fresh, but if it bounces up, it is not and it should not be used.

These days there are any number of specialists who make wonderful sausages and who will ensure delivery almost anywhere.

A recent survey indicated 95% of people enjoyed a cooked breakfast but 94% rarely ate one. However, when people go on holiday they like to start the day with a cooked breakfast, so be prepared to oblige.

TIP

If all else fails, start baking. It fills the house with lovely aromas.

11

The Hospitality Industry and You

The important thing to remember as you start this journey is that you are not alone. You are part of a larger entity called the hospitality industry. Much of your success will be your ability to work co-operatively with others in the industry both here and overseas.

THE STRUCTURE OF TOURISM AUTHORITIES

Each nation's government has its respective **tourism authority** that, in essence, takes responsibility to develop strategies that ensure their share of tourist revenue.

Those registered with their local tourist association may well find they get the majority of their bookings from this source, either by direct bookings through the association or by referring to their official publication.

For the reasons mentioned above, we urge everyone in the Bed & Breakfast industry to join their respective tourism organisation, board or association. In some places, some form of membership is compulsory. The organisation will help you identify why tourists visit your area, to network with other B&B operators, to access local information that helps you make better target market decisions and keeps you up to date with tourism development. Be proactive not reactive.

It is worth noting that a publicly owned company called Tourism Ireland Limited (TIL), has been established by agreement between Bord Fáilte and the Northern Ireland Tourism Board to provide the following services:

- planning and delivering international tourism marketing programmes, including programmes in partnership with the industry north and south;

- publication and dissemination in overseas markets of information of a balanced and comprehensive nature of Ireland as a tourist destination. This must reflect the diverse traditions, forms of cultural expression, and identities within the island;

- market research, provision of information and other appropriate assistance to help the industry develop international marketing expertise;

- co-operation with, consulting and assisting other bodies or associations in carrying out such activities; and

- carrying out surveys and collecting relevant statistics and information.

This newly created company has subsumed the existing Overseas Tourism Marketing Initiative. It will continue to carry out overseas marketing and promotion activity for Bord Fáilte and the Northern Ireland Tourist Board and will establish overseas offices for that purpose.

LOCAL TOURIST ORGANISATIONS

If you have not yet got the picture that you need to be actively involved in the tourism community, we have failed. Your local tourism authority is probably the most important organisation you can join. It will provide you with vital information about your market, but most importantly it will give you vital contacts. Local tourism operators thrive off interaction with each other. It really is a case of you scratch my back and I'll scratch yours.

Destination marketing plays an integral part in the marketing of tourism products. Whether the product is an attraction, activity, scenery, or a Bed & Breakfast, they all, collectively, form the essence of the destination. The more popular the destination, the better are the chances for individual tourism operators to promote and sell their products to potential customers in a cost-effective way.

Destination marketing, promoting the unique brand of a destination, is one of the tasks local or regional tourism organisations are charged with. They prepare the base from which individual operators can undertake their own marketing and promotion at a reduced cost.

Locations such as Lucca, Sienna or Firenze, may not mean a lot to many people, nor would they necessarily associate them with any type of holiday experience. Mention the destination brand, Tuscany, and the story is different. Many will associate that brand not only with a very specific holiday expectation, but they can also place it geographically. In other words, if the destination is known in the marketplace or if it has brand identity, each individual business has the chance of being seen in its marketplace and to reach potential customers faster and at a lower cost.

It should be in everyone's interest, from the smallest B&B operator, to the largest attraction, to ensure that your local and regional tourism organisations receive sufficient support to undertake destination marketing, promote the region and create brand awareness. In return, individual businesses will benefit.

See Useful Addresses for a list of tourism structures for your information, plus other valuable industry contacts.

B&B CLASSIFICATION

There are **national accommodation classification schemes**, which let you know exactly what facilities you need as a Bed & Breakfast host. In all respects, these schemes are designed and implemented by your national tourism centre. Their contact details are listed in Useful Addresses.

Why should you be classified? As more people enter this market the guest is going to become more discerning. Those properties that can advertise their rating will only benefit from it.

Tourism accreditation is a process designed to establish and continually improve industry standards for conducting tourism businesses. It aims to assist every tourism business to improve the way it operates. Listed below are the various national accommodation grading programmes as a guide for your consideration.

England

Serviced and self-catering accommodation
The English Tourism Council has recently introduced a **diamond grading system** for serviced and self-catering guest accommodation.

Properties are rated from 1 to 5 diamonds. The more diamonds, the higher the levels of customer care.

◆   Fair and acceptable

◆◆   Good

◆◆◆   Very good

◆◆◆◆   Excellent*

◆◆◆◆◆   Exceptional, world-class*

                   * You will be guaranteed a wider range of equipment.

Some properties may also obtain a **Gold** or **Silver Award**. These are new and are exclusive to the English Tourism Council. The awards are given to properties that not only achieve the overall quality rating required for their diamond rating, but also reach the highest levels of quality in the areas that guests identify as being really important.

They will reflect the quality of comfort and cleanliness in the bedrooms and the quality of service to be found throughout the stay.

Scotland

Serviced and self-catering accommodation
All visitor accommodation is inspected annually by The Scottish Tourist Board under a statutory system, and all providers, including all the farms listed within this range, offer a high standard.

The Scottish Tourist Board has introduced a new **star scheme** for both serviced and self-catering accommodation where the star award is determined by quality, not by the size of the accommodation or the range of facilities. 'Aim for two stars.'

For self-catering accommodation, the quality standard of the fabric, furnishings, decor, equipment and ambience of the property result in the star awards.

For serviced accommodation the award also takes account of the welcome and service, the food and the hospitality.

Awards range from 1 to 5 stars:

★	Fair and acceptable
★★	Good
★★★	Very good
★★★★	Excellent*
★★★★★	Exceptional, world-class*
	* You will be guaranteed a wider range of equipment.

Wales

Serviced accommodation
The Wales Tourist Board operates a **1–5 star-grading scheme**, which is based on quality. Places that score highly will have an especially welcoming atmosphere and pleasing ambience, and high levels of comfort and guest care. All establishments have been visited and checked by the Wales Tourist Board.

The star grades are:

★	Fair and acceptable
★★	Good
★★★	Very good
★★★★	Excellent
★★★★★	Exceptional, world-class

It is important to bear in mind that the star grade takes into account the nature of the property and the expectation of the guests – so a farmhouse is just as entitled to five stars as a country hotel, as long as what it offers is of the highest standard.

Ireland

Guesthouses, as in other parts of the UK and Ireland, vary from five-bedroom family houses, Georgian and Victorian residences to larger professionally serviced modern premises. The informal atmosphere and personal attention are famous features of this category. The availability of meals to non-residents is not a requirement, however, some provide this service. All guesthouses comply with statutory regulations, which cover physical requirements and the level of service provided. Restaurant facilities are available in some guesthouses.

Four star

This is the top classification for guesthouses in Ireland. All guest bedrooms have private bathrooms with bath and/or shower, direct dial telephone, fax, daily newspaper and colour TV and radio, controllable from the bed. Room service offers full breakfast. Facilities include car parking, safety deposit boxes, fax, newspapers, and baby-sitting service.

Three star

All guest rooms have private bathroom with bath and/or shower, and direct dial telephone. Room service offers breakfast. Facilities include a TV lounge, travellers cheques and at least two major credit cards are accepted.

Two star

Half or more of the guest rooms have private bathroom with bath and/or shower. Facilities include a reading/writing room or lounge area for residents' use.

One star

These premises meet all the mandatory requirements for guesthouses and offer simple accommodation, facilities and services to a satisfactory standard.

Farmhouses

The premises in this category include old-style, period type, and modern farmhouses; the type of farming varies: mixed, tillage, dairy, sheep and poultry – all of interest to visitors, particularly if they come from the city. Evening meals are provided in some houses if notice is given before 12.00 noon each day. A new concept called green tourism, i.e. a holiday experience on a working farm, is also included in this category of accommodation. Irish Farm Holidays Association is the representative body for these premises and further information may be obtained by contacting this pioneering organisation, which is listed under Useful Addresses.

Town and country homes

This category of accommodation covers a variety of houses in urban and rural areas, ranging from the modern bungalow or semi-detached, two-storey house to the large period-style residence. Their main attraction is their homely atmosphere and the opportunity they provide to meet people in their own homes. Some premises provide evening meals if notice is given before 12.00 noon each day.

The Town and Country Homes Association represents members from the above sector.

Specialist accommodation

Specialist accommodation ranges from en suite bedrooms in

country houses to Bed and Breakfast in local homes. It also covers accommodation in pubs.

Northern Ireland

All visitor accommodation is inspected annually by the Northern Ireland Tourist Board under a statutory system introduced in 1948, and all properties listed, including farms, offer a high standard. Full details of requirements and standards may be readily obtained from NITB (see Useful Addresses).

SYMBOLS

Below is a guide to the **symbols** used to indicate the features and facilities available for all the farms listed.

Symbol	Accommodation Type
	Bed & Breakfast
	Self catering
	Bunkhouse
	Camping
	Caravanning

Symbol	Explanation
	Children welcome (minimum age)
	Dogs by arrangement
	Accommodation for disabled/less able people – check for details
	No smoking

Smokers welcome

 Credit cards accepted

 Business people welcome

 Way marked walks on farm

 Foreign languages spoken

 Riding on farm

 Fishing on farm

 Country house, not a working farm

A rating from 1 to 5 stars is the best way for guests to assess the quality of stay that they are looking at. Ratings are an internationally applied yardstick and are administered in this country according to very strict guidelines.

TIP
Being graded gives you an advantage over your competitors.

12

Marketing Your B&B

This chapter is designed to assist you in designing an effective **marketing plan** or concept, for your Bed & Breakfast. This chapter should help you come to decisions on what style of marketing (advertising, promotions, public relations, direct mail, etc) will suit both your customer and your financial situation.

MARKETING CONCEPT

The underpinning factor of your **marketing concept** rests on the importance of guests to your Bed & Breakfast. All of your activities should be aimed at satisfying your guests' needs, while obtaining a profitable, rather than maximum, occupancy.

To develop a marketing concept for your Bed & Breakfast you must:

+ determine the needs of your guests (market research)
+ develop competitive advantages (marketing strategy)
+ select specific markets to serve (target marketing)
+ determine how to satisfy those needs (marketing mix).

MARKET RESEARCH

The fundamentals of operating a successful Bed & Breakfast are the same as running any small business. If you do your homework first then there is less likelihood of coming unstuck.

The aim of **market research** is to find out who your guests are, what they want, where and when they want it.

This research can also expose problems in the way in which you provide products or services, and find areas for expansion of current services to fill customer demand. Market research should also identify trends that can affect bookings and profit levels.

Market research should give you more information than simply who your customers are. Use this knowledge to determine matters such as your market share, the effectiveness of your advertising and promotions, and the response to any new value added services that you have introduced.

While larger companies hire professionals to do their research, small business owners and managers are closer to their customers and are better able to learn much faster the likes and dislikes of their guests. They are better positioned to react quickly to any change in customer preferences.

What to look for
On the basis that you have identified your initial target market, the market research required should investigate four distinct areas:

◆ customers
◆ customer needs
◆ competition
◆ trends.

Some of the things you might like to look at are:

Customers (demographics)

◆ Age.
◆ Income.
◆ Occupation.
◆ Family size.
◆ Marital status.
◆ Country of residence.
◆ Interests and hobbies.

Customer needs

◆ Rest and relaxation.
◆ Is their stay for a limited time, for example, to attend a conference?
◆ Will guests come frequently, for example, business travellers or for sight-seeing?
◆ Are guests looking for a wider experience in your geographical location?

Competition

◆ What is the competition's market share?
◆ How much revenue do you suspect they make?
◆ How many Bed & Breakfasts are targeting the same market?
◆ What attracts customers to them?
◆ What strengths do they advertise?

Trends

◆ Any population shifts.
◆ Changes in local tourism development.
◆ Lifestyle changes in the nearest metro city area.
◆ Short break holidays taken during the week instead of only at weekends.

Where to get information

There are two general sources of information: data already available, and data that can be collected progressively by the Bed & Breakfast operator. The following sources may provide already accessible data:

- The business section of any well-run public library.
- Tourism authorities/local associations.
- Commerce and/or traders' group.
- Professional market research services.

Data can be obtained by the Bed & Breakfast's own research efforts:

- Telephone surveys.
- Local and national newspapers.
- Surveys sent by mail.
- Questionnaires.
- Guest service cards.

Interviewing

Market research does not have to be sophisticated and expensive. While money can be spent in collecting research material, a lot of valuable information can be accessed by the Bed & Breakfast operator using the following methods:

Employees

This is one of the best sources of information about guests' likes and dislikes. Usually employees work more directly with guests and hear complaints that may not make it to the owner. They are also aware of items or services that guests may request, and that the Bed & Breakfast doesn't currently offer.

Guests

Talk to your guests to get a feel for your clientele, and ask them where improvements can be made. Collecting guest comments and suggestions is an effective form of research, as well as instilling customer confidence in your product and property.

Competition

Monitoring the competition can be a useful source of information. Their activities may provide important information about guest demands that you have overlooked. They may be capturing part of the market by offering something unique or different. Likewise, Bed & Breakfast operators can capitalise on unique points of their product that the competition does not offer.

Records and files

Looking at your business records and files can be very informative. Peruse your revenue records, complaints, receipts or any other records that can show you where your guests live or work, or how and what interests them. One Bed & Breakfast operator found that addresses on cash receipts allowed for the pinpointing of guests in a specific geographic area. She thought clients may like to sample the similar, yet different features her area offered.

With this kind of information one can cross-reference the guest addresses and check the effectiveness of the advertising placements. You need to take into account that this material represents the past and the information that you need to determine present and future trends may mean that some past information is too obsolete to be effective, but at least you will have a general idea of what to look for.

MARKETING STRATEGY

With the research information gathered, the next step is to develop a
marketing strategy. Use this information to determine areas where
the competition doesn't adequately fill consumer demand, or to find
areas where a new service or different promotion would capture
part of the market. A new Bed & Breakfast may capture a
significant market share by aiming its marketing strategy on areas
not focused on by the competition.

Some examples of the various areas of emphasis include offering:

- More innovative sight-seeing options.
- Better value for the guests, for example an emphasis on quality.
- Specialised service instead of a broad one.
- Modified facilities, or any improvements.
- A more flexible pricing policy.

While a new Bed & Breakfast can enter this
business and capture a share of the market, an
established one can use the same strategies to
increase its market share.

> **TIP**
> Find ways to fill rooms out of
> season. Put together packages
> with other products' suppliers.

TARGET MARKETING

Once your marketing strategy is developed, you need to determine
with which **customer group** this would be most effective. For
example, a 'value for money' option may be appealing to the family
market while 'quality and top service' would be more attractive to
couples.

Another example could be offering a gift voucher that is set at a
fixed denomination i.e. €100/£100. The person who buys a pre-paid

voucher might present it to a friend or family member as a gift. This allows the holder to use the voucher as payment when checking into your Bed & Breakfast.

Remember that different market strategies may appeal to different target markets. Apply the collected data to choose the combinations that will work best.

The market is defined by different segments. Some examples of this are listed below.

Geographic
Specialise product options to suit guests who live in certain neighbourhoods or regions, or who are from different climates.

Demographic
Direct advertising to families, retired people, the disadvantaged or to the occupation or profession of potential guests.

Special interest groups
Target promotions to the opinions or attitudes of the customers (political or religious, for example).

Product benefits
Aim marketing to emphasise the benefits of the product or service that would appeal to consumers who holiday for this reason (low cost or easy access).

Previous guests
Identify and promote to those guests who have stayed before.

THE MARKETING MIX

Before the marketing mix decision is made, determine what purpose these marketing efforts are going to serve. Are they to:

- deepen the customer base
- increase market share
- increase revenue
- reach new geographic markets, or
- to increase occupancy?

After these objectives are established, determine a date for accomplishing them. The marketing mix allows the Bed & Breakfast to combine different marketing decision areas such as services, promotion and advertising, pricing and place, to construct an overall marketing programme.

PRODUCTS AND SERVICES

Use the **product** or **service** itself as a marketing resource. Having something unique provides motivation behind advertising. While the ideas mentioned under market strategy apply here, another option is to change or modify

> **TIP**
>
> Provide the service you advertise.

the service. Additional attention may be given to a product if it has changed colour, size or style, while a service may draw similar attention by modifying the services provided. Remember sales and promotional opportunities are generated by product differentiation.

PROMOTION AND ADVERTISING

With a marketing strategy and clear objectives outlined, use **advertising** to get the message out to the customers. Advertising can be through:

- The *Yellow* or *Golden Pages.*
- A press release.
- A newspaper.
- Billboards and posters.
- B&B guide books.
- Local tourism publications.
- Direct mail.

The Internet is a relatively cheap way to promote your B&B both domestically and overseas.

One reason to advertise is to highlight promotional activities. This will serve to both highlight your property and offer added incentive for customer patronage. For example you may wish to promote:

- Mid-week, two nights for the price of one offers.
- Coupons or gift vouchers.
- Special activities, eg, mystery-solving evenings.

The aim is to try to reach the largest number of people with the money allocated to advertising and promotion. This may be accomplished by using several different methods of advertising. Be creative and implement ideas.

TIP

Invite local tourist information staff to visit. Give them a complimentary night's stay so they can experience what you have to offer. This can effectively sell your B&B.

Advertising material

The following are some ideas that could help increase the response from your advertising material.

Good quality advertising can be costly, but very rewarding. Again, the emphasis is on 'good'. It's also worth considering full-page advertisements (particularly if you are targeting the luxury market), but after your first year of profitable trade. It is not always appropriate to spend large sums of money in your first year, especially in expensive, national travel magazines, as people don't tend to keep them, and you will have other priorities for your marketing budget.

♦ *Always write the headline from your prospect's point of view not your own.* People tend to not look at their products and services from the perspective of the people buying them. The sooner your prospective guests recognise themselves and their own wants and needs in the words you use in your headline, the faster they will respond.

♦ *Use the words 'You', 'New' and/or 'How to' in your headline.* These are proven words that capture attention. Connect them to a benefit your prospective guests may want, and your response will increase.

♦ *Make your opening sentence continue what you were talking about in the headline.* If in your headline you promised your prospective guest a relaxing stay in your Bed & Breakfast, then say something in your opening sentence about this to get them even more excited about staying with you.

♦ *Tell your whole story, in miniature by the time the first paragraph is over.* People have a very short attention span. Try to telescope your entire story down to a sound bite in writing. Think of how they do this on the TV news, where they give you the key points of an item and then say 'more at 11'. Far more people will read your copy, and the results should produce bookings. Use the rest of your copy to retell your story, in more detail.

◆ *Use specific, powerful and true testimonials.* No matter how honest or persuasive you are, people usually won't believe everything or take everything in as being possible when they first read your copy. They need to get to know you and trust you. That can take some time, but unfortunately you don't want to wait. You have to persuade them right now. They will be much more likely to believe other people when those people are singing your praises. Include testimonials to enhance your credibility.

TIP

Always have a book of photographs and transparencies of your property for unexpected visiting guests.

◆ *Edit your copy ruthlessly.* If a word doesn't keep the reader reading by making your copy more interesting, or what you are selling more appealing, cut it out. Copywriting is the art of doing more with fewer words. Every word has to work really hard, and your copy has to be easy to read.

MARKETING PERFORMANCE

After the marketing mix decision is implemented, the next step is to **evaluate performance**. With a detailed list of your objectives, monitor how well the decisions are developing.

Evaluate objectives such as:

◆ *Market share.* Has the increased share been reached?
◆ *Revenue volume.* Was the increase attained?
◆ *Strategy.* Did the combinations of target markets and strategy work effectively? Which ones didn't?

You should also evaluate the following decisions:

◆ Did the advertising efforts reach target groups?

- Were promotions timely?
- Did customers respond to special offers, coupons or other incentives?

Additionally, consider the following:

- Is your Bed & Breakfast doing all it can to satisfy the guest?

- Is it easy for customers to find what they want at a competitive price?

- If these objectives were not reached, what were the reasons?

- If they worked well, what elements were most effective?

By evaluating performance after decisions have been made, there is reference for future decision-making, based on past results. In addition, periodically assess customer feelings and opinions toward your Bed & Breakfast and how well your guests' needs are being satisfied. This can be done through surveys, customer comments cards, or simply by asking them, 'How did you enjoy your stay?'

Assessing performance and asking for customer input brings us to market research again. Your marketing plan is a continuous effort to identify and adapt to changes in markets, customer taste, and the economy for the success of your Bed & Breakfast.

PUBLIC RELATIONS

All B&Bs have certain things in common: if nothing else you are all dealing with people who are away from their home. Understanding what Bed & Breakfasts have to offer, and the people who patronise them, will play an important part in your marketing approach.

You can quite safely say people frequent Bed & Breakfasts for:

- The personal, pampered feeling they offer.
- The safety and security offered by smaller establishments.
- The opportunity for closer interaction with local surroundings.
- Their suitability for short holiday breaks.

Taking these factors into account you could very well find that **public relations** could offer your Bed & Breakfast your cheapest and most effective form of promotion.

Media relations, where you try to influence journalists and producers of newspapers, magazines, radio shows and TV programmes to do a story on your Bed & Breakfast, at little or no cost, is likely to be the most relevant sector of the PR market. Editorial, as this coverage is known, has more credibility than paid advertising and gives an opportunity to cover more facts.

A **media kit** is the introduction, story, photographs and any other appropriate materials, such as brochures, which you send to the media. The most important component of this kit is the story, or the press release. Used well, a series of press releases can keep your establishment 'in the news'.

Look not only at promoting yourself, but also the attractions of your area, offering your Bed & Breakfast as the most convenient place to stay.

Media releases
The following are some rules to observe when preparing a **press release**.

◆ Write your story considering the questions, 'who, what, why, when, where, and how'. This will help you to include all relevant information.

◆ You must remain focused on what your story is and ensure it appears different from all the other media kits that appear on journalists' desks daily. If it isn't clear to you, it won't be to them.

◆ Restrict your story to one A4 size page. Use your letterhead, as it contains your address and other contact details. Also include your contact name and phone number at the end of your story.

◆ Your media release must be typed with, at least 1 ½ line spacing. Publisher, a Microsoft software program, comes with a format specifically for media releases.

◆ Make your story clear and concise, using simple language. Have a short and punchy title.

◆ Do not exaggerate, tell it like it is. Remember this may appear in print and you have to be able to deliver.

◆ Pay attention to details such as dates and times.

◆ Double check your spelling. This attention to detail is seen as basic courtesy by journalists.

Targeting your story

If your emphasis is on food, naturally food sections of newspapers or gourmet magazines are where your story is best suited. If you offer unique scenery, try the travel section of a weekend paper. If you have gardens that have won awards, then the home or gardening section could be an opportunity.

Prior to writing your release, read the sections you are targeting carefully to understand what it is in each story that captured the imagination of the editor and made it topical.

Get to know your local papers, their deadlines and the names of staff who you will be targeting. Being an active member of your community will enhance your chances of getting a media profile.

A week after posting your media kit follow it up with a phone call. Ask if the media kit has been received. If not, explain briefly what it is about and offer to send another copy. If they have seen it, ask them if they need more information and if they think the story is suitable.

Instead of a traditional media kit you may consider offering journalists and their partners a first hand experience of your Bed & Breakfast. A free night's accommodation is a cheap price to pay for a glowing report in a popular magazine or travel section of a metropolitan newspaper. A journalist's visit will not necessarily provide you with fantastic copy or even an article, but 'freebies' or 'familiarisations' for journalists are part of the system, and word of mouth reports would always be to your advantage. For best effect, limit the period of the offer so journalists are less likely to put it away and forget about you. Good editorial coverage may not make your business, but can provide icing on the cake of your marketing plan. Well done, it is economical and effective.

Public relations are also about relations with your local community. Build up positive relationships with local clubs and business organisations, so you and your business become known and trusted by the locals. Public relations may also include sponsoring a fundraising event, horse race or local sports team for example.

There are a number of books available on how to make public relations work for you. The media unit of your regional tourism association can also provide information and support.

You may wish to consider using a **public relations consultancy** for your initial promotion. You advise the consultant of what you have in mind and your approximate budget, they will come back to you with a proposal. The advantage of a good PR consultancy is that they already have the writing skills and media contacts to make the exercise effective, so your budget can be money well spent.

HOW MUCH MARKETING DO I NEED?

Any expenses incurred in promoting your business can be set against any tax you might pay on your profits, however this can be complicated when you are first embarking upon your venture. Consult your accountant before spending any money. What you should not do is decide that you need a certain type of advertisement just because that's what everyone else does. You must decide what is appropriate to your B&B at any given time. You should, however, have some idea about who it is you are trying to attract and how best to reach them.

A marketing plan and budget needs to be developed in conjunction with your business plan.

BED & BREAKFAST GUIDES

You need to be included in a few Bed & Breakfast **guides** – that is a reality. When you are making your choice you should look at the following:

- How many years has the guide been in existence?
- How many copies does the publisher print?
- How many copies do they actually sell or give away?
- Where is it for sale or distributed?
- How much is it sold for, or is it free?
- How often and when does the guide come out?
- Do you like the method of presentation?
- Do they have a related web site?

How much does it cost?

There are several published Bed & Breakfast & Guesthouse guides you could consider. The following is a list of the more popular guides and contact details and price indications:

Official Guide to Bed & Breakfast guest accommodation (Where to Stay), which is published by:

English Tourism Council
Thames Tower
Blacks Road
Hammersmith
London W6 9EL
Tel: 01242 529509

Only accommodation establishments having applied and paid for a quality rating by English Tourism Council assessors are eligible to appear in *Where to Stay*. Every establishment receives a listing in the directory section of the guides.

In addition, establishments are able to take paid entry in the regional sections – from about £100 for a standard entry (text only) and about £170 for an enhanced entry (includes colour picture and extended description).

Alastair Sawday Publishing – Special Places to Stay
The Home Farm Stables
Barrow Court Lane
Barrow Gurney
Bristol BS48 3RW
Telephone: 01275 464891

This publishing house looks for people and places that they like and that will please a range of guests. They search for special personalities, architecture, furniture, decoration, history, food, general surroundings and gardens. Each B&B (or hotel, or self-catering property) in their guidebooks is a fascinating cocktail of those things and each Alastair Sawday write-up is a reflection of them.

At the heart of their choice of B&Bs is the owner. The finest and most comfortable houses have been turned down because the owner is grumpy or aloof, or the atmosphere cold. Equally, less-than-text-book-perfect houses have been chosen – some may be slightly dusty or chaotic or crumbling – because the owners are so charming they make the place irresistible.

All applicants are subject to inspection and approval by Alastair Sawday Publishing. Although there is a fee for inclusion, it is not possible to simply buy a place in these guides. The entry fee depends on the number of rooms, starting at £335 inc VAT. We suggest you click onto: www.specialplacestostay.com

Bed and Breakfast Nationwide
PO Box 2100
Clacton on Sea
Essex CO16 9BW
Tel: 01255 831235

This brochure is distributed worldwide and features over 640 B&Bs around Britain and Ireland. The majority are family homes with a few guesthouses included in town centres. All the B&Bs have the opportunity to be included on their web site www.bedandbreakfastnationwide.com which is exclusively for properties in the brochure.

They have a policy whereby the listings are limited per location, for example, B&Bs are usually 10–15 miles apart. They only consider extra properties if the number of prospective visitors will satisfy everybody, or hosts are offering accommodation which fits into a different price category.

The publishers visit all listed properties before they are accepted for the brochure.

To give you some idea of the cost of advertising, the fee for 2003 is £280.00 for B&Bs with 3 bedrooms or less (£305.00 for those with 4 + bedrooms). This includes a £30.00 registration fee, which goes towards the cost of visiting you. This fee is only charged in the first year.

AA Bed & Breakfast Guide
AA Hotel Services
Fanum House (15)

Basing View
Basingstoke
Hants RG21 4EA
Tel: 01256 844455

The *AA Bed & Breakfast Guide* is an established market leader, with an estimated 35,000 copies printed every year. This publication is also sold by the American Automobile Association in the USA and is available in Australia – a great global presence. Entries also appear on the AA web site at www.theAA.com

Shown below is an indication of the current Registration and annual fees for inspection and rating, including a listing in the *AA Bed & Breakfast Guide*:

Registration fees

Registration type	Room count	£	2003 fee Inc VAT
Full recognition	1–4	168.00	197.40
	5–10	210.00	246.75
	11 +	240.00	282.00
Associate recognition	1–4	108.00	126.90
	5–10	134.00	157.45
	11 +	160.00	188.00

Annual fees

Registration type	Room count	£	2003 fee Inc VAT
Full recognition	1–4	168.00	197.40
	5–10	210.00	246.75
	11 +	240.00	282.00

Associate recognition	1–4	168.00	197.40
	5–10	210.00	246.75
	11 +	240.00	282.00

TIP

Just because you have your B&B listed in a B&B guide does not mean you can sit back and wait for the phone to ring. There are many operators who have spent thousands of pounds on promoting their business in inappropriate journals with little success.

In the first year of being listed in a **B&B** guide, you will get some bookings, but remember bookshops and newsagencies are going to take all year to sell copies. In the succeeding years, your bookings from this source will increase because the guide will be continually placed in more homes and vehicle glove compartments. Holidaymakers do not usually up-date their accommodation guide every year, but tend to hold on to their copy for a while.

MARKETING PLAN

A **marketing plan** should outline your marketing goals for a twelve-month period and how you expect to achieve them through advertising, promotion, marketing and public relations. You should include the following elements:

- Tourist information centres.
- Direct mail campaigns (including newsletters).
- Public relations (community and media activities).
- Advertising.
- Brochure stationery.
- Business stationery.
- Group promotions.
- Web sites.
- Trade and tourism shows.
- Any other activity that will get your Bed & Breakfast noticed by the public.

Carefully consider any promotional or marketing schemes and opportunities offered to you by your local or regional tourism organisations. The benefits can be considerable.

Your marketing plan will identify your target market and how you plan to reach it.

Do not forget your local community. Word of mouth is the best advertising for any business. Locals will continually be asked for their accommodation recommendations.

Join your local Chamber of Commerce, Rotary or Lions Club. Include membership fees, donations and sponsorships in your marketing plan budget.

Also allow for hidden costs such as photography, artwork design and production. A contingency of 12% will allow for incidentals and price rises for the year.

BROCHURES

Your top marketing priorities will be to ensure that you become involved with your tourist information centre, become part of any local tourist authority initiatives, and create an effective **brochure**.

To enable you to ascertain what will attract your target market, look at your competitors' brochures. Consider what you like, the cost involved, and make it happen.

Remember that you can make a one-colour brochure be as effective as a four-colour brochure if you use the medium carefully. You must ensure your brochure is well written, easy to read, attractive and informative.

NEWSLETTERS

Newsletters are a great way to communicate with your community and with past guests.

Microsoft Publisher has a number of options on template you can adapt for your Bed & Breakfast. These are a great way to create a positive presence in your community and reinforce all the elements of your marketing plan. These newsletters need not be expensive. You can design them on your computer, photocopy them, or even email them to people on your mailing list.

If you include interesting topics and amusing text, they have the opportunity to be passed on to friends. You might want to have the occasional special offer to ascertain effectiveness.

BUSINESS STATIONERY

Your **business stationery** should reflect the design of your brochures and the style of your B&B itself. You need to ensure all of the aspects of promotion are part of one cohesive package.

TIP

Have your letterhead printed on A4 paper, but some on A5 as you are often only sending out short notes.

Get a professional photographer to photograph your B&B. They may cost what is considered a lot of money, but it will be worth it and you'll have the transparencies forever. The photos of your property can be used on your web site, in your brochures and your advertisements.

13

The Fundamentals of Business

N o matter what the financial or personal expectations for your new venture, it is a business and you need to treat it with the gravity it deserves. You will find it impossible to achieve the results you want without a blueprint on how you plan to get there.

In this chapter we aim to give you all the advice you need to get you started in your venture.

Find the notebook we talked about in the first chapter and write down your answers to the following questions:

◆ Do you have any business experience? Write down how you believe you can use this experience in your new business.

◆ Do you have any other experiences you can draw on? How do you believe they will help you?

◆ Have you spoken to an accountant or financial adviser?

◆ Have you contacted your national tourism office or local tourism organisation to get information on your country's tourism statistics?

◆ Have you spoken to your national or regional Bed & Breakfast association? Have you contacted its national office?

◆ Have you determined the financial goals you have for the business?

◆ Have you discussed with your financial adviser the effect that turning your house into a business will have on your financial affairs?

◆ If applicable, have you registered for VAT? Talk to your financial adviser for more information.

◆ Have you looked at various tourism industry publications?

◆ Have you sought the opinions of potential customers and suppliers?

◆ Have you worked out a financial plan to supplement your income while you build your business?

FINANCING

In the first year of your new enterprise you should try to **finance** your venture yourself. However, if additional funding is necessary you need to ensure you contact your small business association, your bank or credit union, or a financial adviser. Remember, all start-up businesses need initial seed capital and B&B is not an exception.

CHOOSING A LEGAL STRUCTURE

Choosing the **legal structure** within which your business will trade is one of the first decisions you will need to make. You must discuss the best options for you with your solicitor and financial adviser.

To prepare you for the meeting, we are providing you with a synopsis of your options. You must not make your final decision based on this, as each business's financial position is different and only your solicitor and your financial adviser have the tools to decide which structure best suits your situation.

It is worth noting at this point that you must be honest with your financial adviser and solicitor about your financial position. They will make the decisions regarding your financial affairs based on the information you give them. If you withhold information it will only be to your financial detriment.

Sole trader

The main advantage of being a **sole trader** is that you are your own boss. The profits are all yours, but so are the losses. You make all the decisions relating to the business yourself – something that can be both a positive and a negative. Tax breaks are usually not as generous. The main disadvantage is that you are personally liable for any business debts, which could put your personal assets at risk.

Partnership

A **partnership** requires two or more people. It has the advantage of pooling resources: financial, experience, brains. It also disperses the risk. Commonly cited disadvantages are disagreements over decision-making and unequal distribution of work. A **partnership agreement** is an essential tool that will clarify from the outset the responsibilities of each partner. The time spent working this out at the beginning of the partnership minimises possible disagreements later. Your solicitor can help you draw up this agreement.

Company

A **company** is a separate entity from its shareholders and as such continues to exist when members change. It is created by incorporation under the Corporations Law. The company structure allows you to separate your personal activities from your business activities. Tax advantages are good but you may still incur personal liability for the liabilities of the company.

Trusts

This is definitely a decision for your financial adviser. **Trusts** are administered by the trustee for the benefit of the beneficiaries of the trust. There are a few different types of trusts and your financial adviser will best be able to advise you of their benefits.

Business names

Be sure to register your business name, for example Mount Tavy Cottage – so as to protect your investment. So, what is a 'business name'? It is a name used by any person, partnership or company and trust for carrying on a business, unless it is the same as their own name. It is advisable to consult a solicitor before using a business name. You should also check local phone books and any relevant trade journals or magazines, to see if any other business is already using the name. If it is, you could face legal difficulties. See the 'Useful Addresses' section at the back of this book for contact points.

WRITING A BUSINESS PLAN

The central point upon which you build your Bed & Breakfast is the **business plan**. Deciding the objectives to pursue during a coming period is an essential factor in realising your dreams, because planning enables you to affect rather than accept the future. Considered planning has positive effects on managerial performance, the quality of work produced, and allows you to think in a contingency-oriented manner.

By definition, a business plan is a written document about your proposed commercial idea and is developed through an identifiable process. It will include an executive summary, a marketing plan, an operational plan and a financial plan.

The main benefits of developing a business plan are:

- It teaches you to forward think.
- It provides data for comparison against actual results.
- It allows providers of credit an insight into your managerial skills.
- It demonstrates that you have investigated the viability of your service in the market place and have an understanding of cash flow.
- It has the potential to demonstrate that your proposed B&B is not viable in your proposed area.

Your business plan should look professional, complete with clearly set out sections that will show the reader that you are organised and capable of running a Bed & Breakfast business.

> **TIP**
>
> No one needs a long-winded business plan. Today, no one is interested in a business plan more than 30 pages long.

The business plan should also assist you in developing an overall perspective of your Bed & Breakfast, determine what markets you are really in, and who your actual competitors are.

Business plan layout

Listed below are the suggested elements that make up a standard Bed & Breakfast business plan.

Table of contents

This is like the contents page in a book. It is a declaration of each subject or chapter and the relevant page number.

Introduction

This should be an overview of who you are and what you hope the document will achieve.

History of B&B in your county or country

This should provide facts and figures, along with a narrative of the history of Bed & Breakfast in your county or country or both.

Why you are going into this B&B business

This should provide a declaration of why you are going into Bed & Breakfast, including what you hope to achieve from it.

Mission statement

Use your mission statement to establish your philosophical goals for the quality your business is offering, for example, customer satisfaction, employee welfare.

Vision statement

A good vision statement can be a critical element in defining your business and is a good opportunity to specifically define what business you are in.

Executive summary

Who are the principals of the business and what is their background? Describe this, as well as what part they will play in the new Bed & Breakfast.

B&B business description

Describe the type of B&B you will be running.

Business aims, objectives and goals

Detail the aims of your business, both personal and financial.

Opportunities for growth

Analysing your market, your proposed service and your product, detail any opportunities there might be for growth over the year and how you intend to capitalise on them.

SWOT analysis

Detail the strengths, weaknesses, opportunities and threats of yourself, your business, and your competitors.

Market analysis

Here is where you detail all the market data you have collected over the previous chapters. You will also detail anything you think will support your enterprise.

Competitor analysis

This is your opportunity to detail your competitors. What they offer that you do not, and vice versa.

Marketing strategy

This is how you plan to target your customers. You have already decided this in prior chapters so you just need to input this information here. You should also detail your pricing policy and competition policy.

Operation plan

This is where you detail your staffing, plant, facility and material requirements. What do you need to run your business day to day?

Financial plan

This is where you add all of your financial analysis. You will need to provide cash flow forecasts, profit and loss statement, balance sheet, and break-even analysis.

Assumptions and risk factors

You need to detail any assumptions that should be made when reading your business plan and any potential risk to your business.

Appendices

List all of your attachments here such as spreadsheets.

Resources available

Seek out Small Business Advisory Centres who are normally located in most towns. Contact your accountant or professional adviser. Your local Chamber of Commerce is a useful body to talk to.

Your business plan is confidential and only shown to your accountant, financial adviser, business partner or bank manager. It's your business's reference point to profitability and peace of mind. There are many publications available that more thoroughly explain how to develop a business plan.

We recommend our companion book *A Business Plan for Bed & Breakfast Owners* by Stewart Whyte with Wal Reynolds – see www.bnb-central.com or www.howtobooks.co.uk

SETTING YOUR ROOM RATE

Having decided what needs to be done in getting your house ready for Bed & Breakfast, you are probably wondering, when you see that mental picture of the property already finished, what your **room rate** should be in the first operating year.

We suggest that you take a calculated guess. Let us assume, for the sake of this exercise, that your guess is £40/€40 per night per room.

Look up a B&B guide and find two properties that already charge £40/€40 per night and book yourself in. Be sure that the two properties are located in a similar environment, but not in the same locality, as yours. For example, if your property is a coastal one then find two others that are also located on the coast.

On checking in, you only need one night in each property, tell the host that you are shortly opening a Bed & Breakfast and that you would be grateful if they could share their experiences with you. Most B&B operators are happy to oblige.

While there, take the opportunity to check the level of hosting and facilities offered for £40/€40 per night. Have a quick look in the guest book and note what comments previous guests have made. You may find that one out of every three remarks relate directly to the intrinsic beauty of the gardens. These comments may be the reason why the B&B is so popular.

After you have stayed in the two selected B&B properties, revisit your own mental picture of your finished B&B and you might find that what you are going to offer could attract a room rate of £50/€50 per night or conversely, £30/€30 per night. In this way, you are going to make a more informed decision.

TIP
Don't underestimate the cost of food when setting your room rate. If you provide a gourmet breakfast you need to make money out of it.

Determining pricing levels and pricing policies is the major factor affecting revenue. Factors such as demand, the market price, and customer responsiveness to price changes, influence the price levels.

Other factors such as a convenient location or a more personalised service may allow a Bed & Breakfast to charge a higher room rate.

Market mix

Now we get to the fun part. Let us assume that your proposed room rate is £40/€40 per night and that you have three guest rooms, all with their own en suites, and priced the same.

Now we assume that in the first operating year your occupancy rate is targeted at 40%. That means we have approximately 21 weeks of projected bookings. 147 days × three guestrooms equals 441 room nights. If every booking was worth £40/€40 then the annual turnover would be £17,640/€17,640.

But will all of your bookings be direct? You need to now consider **market mix**, which is to suggest that your bookings may come from different sources that attract different levels of pricing. In the table shown, we list the various booking sources, and room rates they could attract.

Booking source	Room nights sold (No)	Percentage share (%)	Room rate charged (£)(€)	Receipts (£) (€)
Direct	265 bed nights	60	40	10,600
Off peak	44	10	35	1,540
Corporate	44	10	30	1,320
Internet	66	15	40	2,640
T/Operator	22	5	30	656
Total	441	100	38	16,756

In this example, actual receipts show that the average room rate was £38/€38 per night not £40/€40 as first thought. This demonstrates the effect of market mix. Ideally, you do some research in order to gauge where your bookings are likely to originate and budget accordingly.

If you find that the vast majority of bookings originate from sources that attract a low room rate then you may wish to adjust your marketing strategy and in turn your projected profit and loss figures. Don't forget seasonal factors.

TAXATION AND THE BED & BREAKFAST BUSINESS

As in most small enterprises, there is a range of **business tax regulations** governing the running of a Bed & Breakfast. Rules governing the business rate payments by guest accommodation establishments have been in place for some years, however, the rigorous approach in recent times taken by the valuation offices has become a significant factor in many local economies.

So what are business rates?

Business rates are a national tax on the occupation of non-domestic property paid to, and administered by, central government although the revenue is used to provide local services. With a few specific exceptions, each non-domestic property has a rateable value, which is based on the market rent it would be expected to command. A B&B property is deemed domestic and therefore subject to normal council tax in some places, rather than business rates if:

◆ you intend not to provide short stay accommodation for more than six people at any one time in the coming year, or

◆ the property is your sole residence and the Bed & Breakfast use is subsidiary to the private use.

As a rough guide, if half or more of the whole house (not just bedrooms) is devoted to B&B guests at anyone time, then the property is likely to be business rated. We suggest strongly that you consult with your accountant or tax agent as to your true position.

Capital gains tax

When you sell a property you may have to pay **capital gains tax** (CGT) – not on the whole amount you sell it for, but on the gain you make in selling it. However, there are various tax reliefs available. See leaflet CGT1 'Capital gains tax'.

VAT

If **VAT** is applicable, there is much your business will need to do to ensure it is compliant. The other concern for you and your liability is that you are turning, in most cases, your family home into a business. **You will need very good taxation advice prior to taking in your first guest.** Make this a top priority.

COMPUTER LITERACY

Computers have become an important factor in our daily lives. Everywhere we go there seems to be a computer involved, be it when banking, visiting a doctor or dentist and at the check-out counters of any supermarket or department store.

School children are been taught how to use computers as part of their education. Typewriters are now something out of a bygone era. We now depend on computers to operate a vast range of software programs that enable us to more effectively run our business.

It is important, therefore, that all of society accepts the challenge and become computer literate. Not to do so can inhibit one from having more say in the knowledge-based information era that we all now live in.

Throughout the country, there are many locally-based learning faculties or tertiary colleges, which run introduction or beginner computer courses at very competitive rates.

If you have not already done so you should enrol yourself in one now. The longer you leave becoming technologically literate, the more difficult it is going to be.

PURCHASING A COMPUTER
The bottom line here is to purchase the best you can afford. It's true that computers become cheaper every day and the computer you buy today will be outdated, if not tomorrow, in around a year.

If you buy the best you can afford now it is likely to be around for longer, even as technology surpasses it. It is not a case of waiting until the upgrading of computers stops. That is not going to happen soon and it would be a false economy to purchase one with this in mind. The bottom line is, it is almost impossible to do business today without the use of a computer.

When you are making your purchase ensure that you get the fastest modem you can afford. Do take the advice of a knowledgeable specialist you trust.

THE INTERNET
During the past 30 years very few people would have considered doing business without having access to a telephone and, during the last fifteen years, most businesses would consider it essential to have a facsimile machine. In many businesses today the Internet is already an essential tool, and it will not be long before this extends to all areas and types of businesses.

Telephones have been with us long enough for people to consider them as a natural extension of communication using the voice. The fax machine followed on from the mail system as a natural extension of the written word. A computer, with connection to the **Internet**, has the capability to extend all areas of audio, visual and written communication.

It can be used as an alternative to the phone, for online communication and, in the form of email, replace or supplement the use of the fax machine. It can be used to replace photographs, videos and live audiovisual connections. This area of communications is just the tip of the iceberg. The Internet is revolutionising almost every aspect of human endeavour. Areas affected include advertising, entertainment, education, reference material and shopping. The list goes on and on. One of the prime areas it has revolutionised is travel.

With the Internet, many people are at the same stage as a child picking up a telephone receiver for the first time to say 'hello'. It's a steep learning curve, and one that a lot of us think we would rather not climb. At present the Internet is a tool that can help us thrive in business, but in future it will be a tool that we will need to survive in business.

SEARCH ENGINES

Whether you believe that the Internet is of real value to those in B&Bs, or just plain old hype, there is one point upon which most of us will agree: a lot of information can be found on the Internet. We can most likely agree that information is a key input to any business process. In fact, it's the availability of information, not the lure of making money on the Net that should take first priority for Bed & Breakfast owners as they merge into Internet traffic.

While there are several ways to find and distribute information on the Internet, for example mailing lists and email, the most accessible is the World Wide Web. But because there is no central depository for storing, locating, and retrieving web documents, the system would be useless without the search tools that give users an opportunity of finding the information they want.

It is important for B&B operators to understand how search tools operate. A working knowledge of common search tools will help you save time, find hidden opportunities, avoid mistakes caused by lack of information, and make your Internet marketing efforts more productive.

There are several good sources of information about search tools that can be found in public libraries and tertiary colleges, many of which run short courses on this subject. Different information sources are directed toward different types of users: researchers, library professionals, web marketers and web developers.

The focus of this information is of interest to B&B owners as you try to make the most of what the Internet has to offer.

The objective is to:

◆ Provide general information about search tools.
◆ Provide some basic searching tips.
◆ Provide ideas for creating 'search friendly' web sites.

Search tools seem rather straightforward. You go to a search site such as Yahoo! or Bullseye, type in a keyword or two and it returns descriptions of web documents that meet your search criteria. Unfortunately, like so many other aspects of the Internet, searching for information is both easy and difficult to do. There are several reasons for this:

◆ Different types of searches require different search tools.

◆ Search procedures vary among different search tools.

◆ Different search tools will yield different results from identical queries.

◆ It is often necessary to use more than one search tool to get reliable results.

◆ The syntax of a search may dramatically affect results.

◆ Simple searches will often yield thousands of documents that satisfy the search criteria.

If your intention is to develop your own **web site**, then knowledge about search tools is important for other reasons. Much of the traffic to your site will come from directories and search engines. Decisions you make about content and design will affect the likelihood of potential guests visiting your site. Therefore, this is not an issue that should be left entirely up to the web designer or a submission service. You must understand how and why visitors will find your site in order to influence that process.

The term 'search engine' is often used as a catchall phrase for search tools. It is more accurate to use 'search engine' to describe one type of search tool and 'directory' to describe the other. The confusion stems from the fact that both types enable users to search an index or database. The difference is in the way the index is created.

People who review web sites and categorise them by subject, create directory indexes. Search engines are used by specialised software tools to automatically visit sites and index their contents. Web sites are submitted to a directory for review and either included within one or more categories or rejected by the reviewer.

Because of the human element involved, directory indexes are much smaller than search engine indexes (thousands of pages versus millions of pages).

Users find information by either:

- ◆ moving through progressively narrower categories, or
- ◆ using the directory's 'search' capacity.

A directory search generally involves entering one or more keywords. The directory will then return a list of categories that contain relevant sites, or of individual web sites that contain one or more of the keywords, or a combination of both. The list will not necessarily be in any particular order.

Software programs called 'robots' compile search engine indexes. Generally, either the site's creator or a submission service submits web site addresses, or URLs. This prompts a robot to visit the site and index most, or all, of the site text.

Search engine users find information by performing a keyword search, but while a simple search capability is adequate for a directory, sophisticated techniques may be needed to retrieve meaningful results from a large search engine database.

Since each search engine has its own index, a given site may be indexed by some search engines and not others. Different search engines use different formulas to find web pages that match the user's query, and then rank the matching pages according to relevance. Resubmitting your web site to the numerous search engines is one way of making sure you appear early in the list of properties displayed. There are now people who specialise in providing just that service.

It is therefore possible to enter the same search criteria into two different search engines and receive two different sets of results.

CREATING A WEB PAGE

The best way to go about creating a **web page** is to spend time studying the web, looking at as many pages as possible and determining what works and what doesn't. Buy a WYSIWYG editor, similar to FrontPage98, as they have useful tutorials and samples.

When you see a page you like that someone else has done, save it and learn the HTML coding so you know how it was done. You can then adapt the same for your own requirements.

On the web there are many sites that have tutorials and explanations of every aspect of web site design and implementation. Read reviews of books on the Internet for hints and tips. Spend time on your site and experiment. Create a style. Keep it simple and start small as you can always make it striking and involved later on.

Publish and announce your site to friends, search engines and directories, but most of all refine the site and widen your goals and learning experiences. It may well be that the best option is to hook onto a community web site or source local directories to appear on. Seek local advice, as with every aspect of your B&B business.

Your web design must reflect your goals and once those needs have been identified and an agreed structure is in place, then the site design and construction can commence. This process is very different

TIP

Knowledge is power!

from designing a newspaper advertisement, which can remain static, as it needs to be maintained and updated at regular intervals.

Be sure that you clearly determine the goals of your Bed & Breakfast site. Is the goal to provide a service, list your property or to supply some other service such as an index or registry? Visitors to your site will be looking for the listed material:

◆ Who are the hosts?
◆ What facilities do you offer?
◆ What are your room rates?
◆ How can you be contacted?
◆ Why should I stay at your B&B instead of someone else's?
◆ Can I book directly from the site?
◆ What is the availability like on my required dates?

Make sure that your web site is easy to navigate, thus allowing everyone to find you. Have navigation buttons or text with informative descriptions that enables the visitor to know where they are going and what to expect.

Have a contents page that lists the features of your Bed & Breakfast site, and be sure it's interesting enough to ensure a return visit.

Visual aids, particularly for accommodation, are very important. Have a photographer take very good photos of your establishment.

A well-designed web site can become an effective marketing and selling tool for your Bed & Breakfast. If you don't feel up to the challenge of designing it yourself there is an abundance of web designers who will design one for you for fees ranging from the very high to the very low.

But beware, like everything else, your web site must have a professional appearance if you're not going to waste your money. Be careful whom you choose to set up your site. There are charlatans who will charge thousands for a service that shouldn't cost more than two or three hundred at the very most. Ask to see examples of their work and the 'hits' they are attracting (the number of people who look at the sites and the average time spent on it). In the future, it could well become the major instrument for generating bookings.

Again, research will pay dividends. Once your web site is up and running you will need to make sure people can find it.

CHOOSING AN INTERNET PROVIDER

When connecting to the Internet, be sure to shop around for the deal that matches your needs. Firstly, estimate the number of hours per month you are most likely to be on the net along with the amount of download time. We suggest that you start out with a modest number of hours and download time, as you should be able to alter the terms of your arrangement with the chosen **service provider**.

Approximately 574 million people were connected to the Internet world wide web as at the commencement of 2003 and this number is expected to increase to 1,000,000,000 by the year 2005, with that number growing by about 3% per month. Currently, an estimated 42% of all UK households (10.5 million) are connected to the Internet with 47 million European household expected to be on this year. An estimated 35% of all those people who have Internet access will buy travel related products this year. Are you ready?

Glossary

Account balance The difference between the total debits and total credits of an account.

À la carte Where the guest can order anything on a vast menu and only pays for what she/he eats.

Artwork This is the name given to original material, photographs, illustrations, typesetting (lettering) etc, when making up the overall design of a printing job.

Assets Things of value owned by a person or business.

Bad debt A loss caused by the failure of a customer to pay for what is owed.

Balance sheet A statement at a certain date, setting out the assets, liabilities and proprietorship of a business.

Bookkeeping The systematic recording of financial transactions in a journal, then a ledger, then a trial balance.

Camera ready artwork Is artwork prepared to a stage from which a printing plate can be made without further changes.

Capital The wealth, including money and property used in the business.

Commission Percentage of sale paid as a fee to an agent selling your accommodation.

Cost of goods sold The cost of producing, converting or acquiring goods sold during a period.

Cover Place or setting at a table. Term used by waiting staff.

Creditor One to whom money is owed by your business.

Debtor One who owes money to your business.

Email See **Internet**.

Expenditure Costs and charges of operating a business which decrease profits.

Franchise A contract under which a party is licensed by another to use a name, product, service or business system, in return for a fee.

Goodwill An intangible asset which includes business reputation, an established trading level, favourable location, licensing or exclusive trading rights.

HTML Hyper Text Mark-up Language.

Inbound tourism Travellers who are coming to your country from overseas.

Industrial award Terms and conditions of employment negotiated and agreed on by employers, government and union representatives.

Internet International computer network using phone lines (accessed by a box called a modem). The Internet includes a personal message service (email).

Invoice Document showing details of the charges for goods sold or service provided on account.

Invoicing period A regular time period after which invoices are issued for all sales made or services provided during that period. Normally 7 or 30 days.

Journal A book of first entry in which financial transactions are entered as they occur.

Ledger A book in which financial transactions are classified in various accounts.

Liabilities Amounts owed by a person or business, including loans and outstanding debts.

Outbound tourism Travellers who reside in your country and are leaving for overseas for their holiday.

Owners equity The value of the person after liabilities have been deducted from assets. This is the amount of money that would be distributed to the owners if the business entity were dissolved.

Rack rate The price at which you advertise your Bed & Breakfast.

Revenue Income from business transactions.

Table d'hôte Refers to a set menu at a set price.

Trading hours Open for business.

Trading terms The terms of business applied to creditors, eg invoices due for payment within 7 days of issue.

Working capital The capital or assets required to fund the daily operation of the business on a short-term basis. It is calculated by deducting current liabilities from current assets.

WWW World Wide Web. The user's name for the Internet. WWW is included in all addresses (like phone numbers and extensions) on the Internet. Also known as URL.

Useful Addresses

ENGLAND

English Tourism Council, Thames Tower, Black's Road, London W6 9EL.
Tel: +44 (0) 208 563 3000 Fax: +44 (0) 208 563 3234
Email: comments@englishtourism.org.uk

Regional tourist boards
Cumbria Tourist Board (CTB), Ashleigh, Holly Road, Windermere, Cumbria
LA23 2AQ. Tel: (015394) 44444 Fax: (015394) 44041
Web site: www.golakes.co.uk
(Covering Cumbria and The Lake District)

East of England Tourist Board (EETB), Toppesfield Hall, Hadleigh, Suffolk IP7
5DN. Tel: (01473) 822922 Fax: (01473) 823063
Web site: www.eastofenglandtouristboard.com
(Covering Cambridgeshire, Essex, Hertfordshire, Bedfordshire, Norfolk and
Suffolk)

Heart of England Tourist Board (HETB), Woodside, Larkhill Road, Worcester
WR5 2EZ. Tel: (01905) 763436 Fax: (01905) 763450
Web site: www.hetb.co.uk (business) www.visitheartofengland.com (visitor)
(Covering Derbyshire, Gloucestershire, Leicestershire, Lincolnshire,
Northamptonshire, Nottinghamshire, Shropshire, Staffordshire,
Warwickshire, Hereford and Worcester, West Midlands)

London Tourist Board (LTB), 1 Warwick Row, London SW1P 5ER. Tel: (020)
7932 2000 Fax: (020) 7932 0222. Web site: www.londontouristboard.com
(Covering Greater London)

Northumbria Tourist Board (NTB), Aykley Heads, Durham DH1 5UX.
Tel: (0191) 375 3000 Fax: (0191) 386 0899.
Web site: www.e-northumbria.net (business)
(Covering Durham, Northumberland, the Tees Valley and Tyne and Wear)

North West Tourist Board (NWTB), Swan House, Swan Meadow Road,
Wigan Pier, Wigan WN3 5BB. Tel: (01942) 821222 Fax: (01942) 820002.
Web site: www.nwtourism.net (business)
(Covering Cheshire, Greater Manchester, Lancashire, Merseyside)

South East of England Tourist Board (SEETB), The Old Brew House, Warwick
Park, Tunbridge Wells, Kent TN2 5TU. Tel: (01892) 540766 Fax: (01982)
511008 Web site: www.tourismsoutheast.com (business)
(Covering East and West Sussex, Kent, and Surrey)

Southern Tourist Board (STB), 40 Chamberlayne Road, Eastleigh, Hampshire
SO50 5JH. Tel: (023) 8062 5400 Fax: (023) 8062 0010.
Web site: www.southerntb.co.uk (business)
(Covering Berkshire, East Dorset, Hampshire, Isle of Wight, Buckinghamshire,
Oxfordshire)

South West Tourism (SWT) (formerly West Country Tourist Board (WCTB)),
Woodwater Park, Pynes Hill, Rydon Lane, Exeter EX2 5WT. Tel: (0870) 442
0830 Fax: (0870) 442 0840. Web site: www.swtourism.co.uk (business)
(Covering Bath, Bristol, Cornwall and the Isles of Scilly, Devon, West Dorset,
Somerset, Wiltshire)

Yorkshire Tourist Board (YTB), 312 Tadcaster Road, York YO24 1GS. Tel:
(01904) 707961 Fax: (01904) 701414. Web site:
www.yorkshiretouristboard.net (business)
Covering Yorkshire, North Lincolnshire and North East Lincolnshire)

Farm Stay UK, C/o Farm Stay UK Ltd, National Agricultural Centre, Stoneleigh Park, Warwickshire CV8 2LZ. Tel: +44 (0)24 7669 6909 Fax: +44 (0)24 7669 6630. Email: enquiries@farmstayUK.co.uk

IRELAND

Northern Ireland Tourist Board, St Anne's Court, 59 North Street, Belfast BT1 1NB. Tel: (028) 9023 1221 Fax: (028) 9024 0960.
Web site: www.nitb.com

Causeway Coast and Glens Ltd, 11 Lodge Road, Coleraine, Co Londonderry, BT52 1LU. Tel: (028) 7032 7720 Fax: (028) 7032 7719
Web site: www.causewaycoastandglens.com

Belfast Visitor and Convention Bureau, 47 Donegall Place, Belfast BT1 5AD. Tel: (028) 9024 6609 Fax: (028) 9031 2424. Web site: www.gotobelfast.com

Derry Visitor and Convention Bureau, 44 Foyle Street, Derry BT48 6AT. Tel: 028 7137 7577. Web site: www.derryvisitor.com

Kingdoms of Down, 40 West Street, Newtownards, BT23 4EN. Tel: (028) 9182 2881 Fax: (028) 9182 2202. Web site: www.kingdomsofdown.com

Fermanagh Lakeland Tourism, Wellington Road, Enniskillen, Co Fermanagh, BT74 7EF. Tel: (028) 6634 6736 Fax: (028) 6632 5511

Bord Fáilte Eireann, Baggot Street Bridge, Baggot St, Dublin 2, Ireland. Tel: 01850 23 03 30. Fax: 01 60 24 100. Email: user@irishtouristboard.ie.
Web site: www.ireland.travel.ie

Tourism Accommodation Approvals Ltd., Coolcholly, Ballyshannon, Co Donegal, Ireland. Tel: 072 52 760 Fax: 072 52 761 Email:
taahome@eircom.net

Town and Country Homes, Belleek Road, Ballyshannon, Co Donegal, Ireland. Tel: 071 98 222 22. Fax: 071 98 222 07. Email: admin@townandcountry.ie.

Web site: www.townandcountry.ie WAP: www.bandbireland.com

Irish Farmhouse Holidays Association, 2 Michael Street, Limerick, Ireland. Tel: 061 400 700. Fax: 061 400 771. Web site: www.irishfarmholidays.com. Email: farmhols@ioi.ie

Belfast
Bord Fáilte, 53 Castle Street, Belfast BT1 1GH. Tel: 00 44 28 9032 7888 Fax: 00 44 28 9024 0201

Dublin Tourism Centre, Suffolk Street, Dublin 2.
Web site: www.visitdublin.com

South West Tourism (Cork, South Kerry)
Aras Fáilte, Grand Parade, Cork, Ireland. Tel: +353 21 4255100 Fax: +353 21 4255199. Web site: www.corkkerry.ie

Ireland West Tourism (Galway, Mayo, Roscommon)
Aras Fáilte, Forster Street, Galway, Ireland. Tel: +353 91 537700 Fax: +353 91 537733

East Coast & Midlands Tourism (Kildare, Laois, Longford, Louth, Meath, North Offaly, Westmeath, Wicklow)
Market House, Mullingar, Co Westmeath, Ireland. Tel: +353 44 48650 Fax: +353 44 40413. Web site: www.ecoast-midlands.travel.ie

North West Tourism (Counties Cavan, Donegal, Leitrim, Monaghan and Sligo)
Aras Redden, Temple Street, Sligo. Tel: +353 71 61201 Fax: +353 71 60360. Web site: www.ireland-northwest.travel.ie

Shannon Development (for counties Clare, Limerick, North Kerry, North Tipperary and South Offaly)
Shannon Airport Tourist Office, Shannon Airport, Shannon, Co Clare. Tel: +353 61 471664 Fax: +353 61 471661

South East Tourism (Carlow, Kilkenny, South Tipperary, Waterford and Wexford) 41 The Quay, Waterford, Ireland. Tel: +353 51 875823 Fax: +353 51 877388 Web site: www.southeastireland.com

SCOTLAND

VisitScotland, 23 Ravelston Terrace, Edinburgh EH4 3TP. Tel: (0131) 332 2433 Web site: www.visitscotland.com and www.scotexchange.net

Regional Tourist Offices

Aberdeen and Grampian

Aberdeen & Grampian Tourist Board, 27 Albyn Place, Aberdeen AB10 1YL. Tel: +44 (01224) 288800 (admin). Web site: www.castlesandwhisky.com

Angus and Dundee

Angus & Dundee Tourist Board, 21 Castle Street, Dundee DD1 3AA. Tel: +44 (01382) 527540 (CE). Web site: www.angusanddundee.co.uk

Argyll, the Isles, Loch Lomond, Stirling and the Trossachs (AILLST)

Old Town Jail, St John Street, Stirling FK8 1EA. Tel: +44 (01786) 445222 (admin). Web site: www.scottish.heartlands.org

Ayrshire & Arran

Ayrshire Tourist Board, Block 2, 15 Skye Road, Prestwick KA9 2TA. Tel: +44 (01292) 470700 (admin). Web site: www.ayrshire-arran.com

Dumfries and Galloway

Dumfries & Galloway Tourist Board, 64 Whitesands, Dumfries DG1 2RS. Tel: +44 (01387) 245550 (headquarters).
Web site: www.dumfriesandgalloway.co.uk/

Edinburgh and Lothians

Edinburgh & Lothians Tourist Board, 4 Rothesay Terrace, Edinburgh EH3 7RY Tel: +44 (0131) 473 3600. Web site: www.edinburgh.org/

Greater Glasgow and Clyde Valley
Greater Glasgow and Clyde Valley Tourist Board, 11 George Square, Glasgow G2 1DY. Tel: +44 (0141) 204 4480 (admin). Web site: www.seeglasgow.com

Highlands of Scotland
The Highlands of Scotland Tourist Board, Peffery House, Strathpeffer IV14 9HA Tel: +44 (01997) 421160. Web site: www.host.co.uk

Kingdom of Fife
Kingdom of Fife Tourist Board, Haig House, Haig Business Park, Markinch KY7 6AQ. Tel: (01592) 750066. Web site: www.standrews.com/fife

Orkney
Orkney Tourist Board, 6 Broad Street, Kirkwall, Orkney KW15 1NX. Tel: +44 (01856) 872001 (admin). Web site: www.visitorkney.co

Perthshire
Perthshire Tourist Board, Lower City Mills, West Mill Street, Perth PH1 5QP. Tel: +44 (01738) 627958. Web site: www.perthshire.co.uk

Scottish Borders
Scottish Borders Tourist Board, Shepherds Mills, Whinfield Road, Selkirk TD7 5DT. Tel: +44 (01750) 20555 (admin).

Shetland Islands
Shetland Islands Tourism, Market Cross, Lerwick, Shetland ZE1 0LU. Tel: +44 (01595) 693434. Web site: www.shetland-tourism.co.uk

The Western Isles
Western Isles Tourist Board, 4 South Beach, Stornoway, Isle of Lewis HS1 2XY Tel: +44 (01851) 701818 (admin). Web site: www.witb.co.uk

WALES

Wales Tourist Board, Brunel House, 2 Fitzalan Rd, Cardiff CF2 1UY. Tel: (029) 2049 9909 Fax: (029) 2047 5321. Web site: www.wales-tourist-board.gov.uk

The Isle of Anglesey
Holyhead Tourist Information Centre, Stenna Line, Terminal 1 Holyhead, Anglesey LL65 1DQ. Tel: 01407 762622 Fax: 01407 761462

Llanfairpwllgwyngyll Tourist Information Centre, Station Site, Llanfairpwllgwyngyll, Anglesey LL61 5UJ. Tel: 01248 713177 Fax: 01248 715711

Llandudno, Colwyn Bay, Rhyl and Prestatyn
Conwy Tourist Information Centre, Conwy Castle Visitor Centre, Conwy LL32 8LD. Tel: 01492 592248 Fax: 01492 573545

Llandudno Tourist Information Centre, 1–2 Chapel Street, Llandudno, Gwynedd LL30 2YU. Tel: 01492 876413 Fax: 01492 872722

Rhos on Sea Tourist Information Centre, The Promenade, Rhos on Sea, Conwy LL28 4EP. Tel: 01492 548778 Fax: 01492 548778

Colwyn Bay Tourist Information Centre, Imperial Buildings, Station Square, Princes Drive, Colwyn Bay, Conwy LL29 8LF. Tel: 01492 530478 Fax: 01492 534789

Rhyl Tourist Information Centre, Rhyl Children's Village, West Parade, Rhyl, Denbighshire LL18 1HZ. Tel: 01745 355068 Fax: 01745 342255

The North Wales Borderlands
Mold Tourist Information Centre, Library Museum & Art Gallery, Earl Road, Mold CH7 1AP. Tel: 01352 759331 Fax: 01352 759331

Wrexham Tourist Information Centre, Lambpit Street, Wrexham LL11 1WN. Tel: 01978 292015 Fax: 01978 292467

Llangollen Tourist Information Centre, Town Hall, Castle Street, Llangollen, Denbighshire LL20 5PD. Tel: 01978 860828 Fax: 01978 861563

Ruthin Tourist Information Centre, Ruthin Craft Centre, Park Road, Ruthin, Denbighshire LL15 1BB. Tel: 01824 703992 Fax: 01824 703992

Snowdonia Mountains and Coast
Aberdyfi Tourist Information Centre, The Wharf Gardens, Aberdyfi, Gwynedd LL35 0ED. Tel: 01654 767321 Fax: 01654 767321

Bala Tourist Information Centre, Penllyn, Pensarn Road, Bala, Gwynedd LL23 7SR. Tel: 01678 521021 Fax: 01678 521021

Bangor Tourist Information Centre, Town Hall, Deiniol Road, Bangor, Gwynedd LL57 2R. Tel: 01248 352786 Fax: 01248 352786

Barmouth Tourist Information Centre, The Old Library, Station Road, Barmouth Gwynedd LL42 1LU. Tel: 01341 280787 Fax: 01341 280787

Beddgelert Tourist Information Centre, Canolfan Hebog, Beddgelert, Gwynedd LL55 4YD. Tel: 01766 890615 Fax: 01766 890615

Betws y Coed Tourist Information Centre, Royal Oak Stables, Betws y Coed Conwy LL24 0AH. Tel: 01690 710426 Fax: 01690 710665

Blaenau Ffestiniog Tourist Information Centre, Unit 3, High Street, Blaenau Ffestiniog, Gwynedd LL41 3HS. Tel: 01766 830360 Fax: 01766 830360

Caernarfon Tourist Information Centre, Oriel Pendeitsh, Castle Street, Caernarfon, Gwynedd LL55 1ES. Tel: 01286 672232 Fax: 01286 678209

Corris Tourist Information Centre, Corris Craft Centre, Corris, Gwynedd SY20 9RF. Tel: 01654 761244 Fax: 01654 761244

Dolgellau Tourist Information Centre, Ty Meirion, Eldon Square, Dolgellau, Gwynedd LL40 1PU. Tel: 01341 422888 Fax: 01341 422576

Harlech Tourist Information Centre, Penygongl, 1 High Street, Harlech, Gwynedd LL46 2YE. Tel: 01766 780658 Fax: 01766 780658

Llanberis Tourist Information Centre, 41b High Street, Llanberis, Gwynedd LL55 4EU. Tel: 01286 870765 Fax: 01286 871924

Machynlleth Tourist Information Centre, Canolfan Owain Glyndwr, Machynlleth, Powys SY20 8EE. Tel: 01654 702401 Fax: 01654 703675

Porthmadog Tourist Information Centre, High Street, Porthmadog, Gwynedd LL49 9LD. Tel: 01766 512981 Fax: 01766 515312

Pwllheli Tourist Information Centre, Min y Don, Station Square, Pwllheli, Gwynedd LL53 5HG. Tel: 01758 613000 Fax: 01758 613000

Tywyn Tourist Information Centre, High Street, Tywyn, Gwynedd LL36 9AD Tel: 01654 710070 Fax: 01654 710070

Mid Wales and the Brecon Beacons
Llanidloes Tourist Information Centre, 54 Longbridge Street, Llanidloes, Powys SY18 6EF. Tel: 01686 412605 Fax: 01686 413884

Crickhowell Tourist Information Centre, Beaufort Chambers, Beaufort Street Crickhowell, Powys NP8 1AA. Tel: 01873 812105

Machynlleth Tourist Information Centre, Canolfan Owain Glyndwr, Machynlleth, Powys SY20 8EE. Tel: 01654 702401 Fax: 01654 703675

Brecon Tourist Information Centre, Cattle Market Car Park, Brecon, Powys LD3 9DA. Tel: 01874 622485 Fax: 01874 625256

Knighton Tourist Information Centre, Offas Dyke Centre, West Street, Knighton Powys LD7 1EN. Tel: 01547 529424

Llandrindod Wells Tourist Information Centre, Old Town Hall, Memorial Gardens, Llandrindod Wells, Powys LD1 5DL. Tel: 01597 822600 Fax: 01597 829164

Builth Wells Tourist Information Centre, The Groe Car Park, Builth Wells, Powys LD2 3BT. Tel: 01982 553307 Fax: 01982 553841

Presteigne Tourist Information Centre, The Judge's Lodging, Broad Street Presteigne, Powys LD8 2AD. Tel: 01544 260650 Fax: 01544 260652

Rhayader Tourist Information Centre, The Leisure Centre, North Street, Rhayader, Powys LD6 5BU. Tel: 01597 810591

Newtown Tourist Information Centre, The Park Back Lane, Newtown, Powys SY16 2PW. Tel: 01686 625580 Fax: 01686 610065

Llanwrtyd Wells Tourist Information Centre, Ty Barcud, The Square, Llanwrtyd Wells, Powys LD5 4RB. Tel: 01591 610666 Fax: 01591 610666

Lake Vyrnwy Tourist Information Centre, Unit 2, Vyrnwy Craft Workshops, Lake Vyrnwy, Powys SY10 0LY. Tel: 01691 870346 Fax: 01691 870346

Welshpool Tourist Information Centre, Vicarage Garden, Church Street, Welshpool, Powys SY21 7DD. Tel: 01938 552043 Fax: 01938 554038

Ceredigion
Borth
Cambrian Terrace, Borth, Ceredigion SY24 5HY. Tel: 01970 871174 Fax: 01970 871365

New Quay
Church Street, New Quay, Ceredigion SA45 9NZ. Tel: 01545 560865 Fax: 01970 626566

Aberystwyth
Terrace Road, Aberystwyth, Ceredigion SY23 2AG. Tel: 01970 612125 Fax: 01970 612125

Aberaeron

The Quay, Aberaeron, Ceredigion SA46 0BT. Tel: 01545 570602 Fax: 01545 571534

Cardigan

Theatr Mwldan, Bath House Road, Cardigan, Ceredigion SA43 2JY. Tel: 01239 613230 Fax: 01239 614853

Pembrokeshire
Newport (Pembs)

2 Bank Cottages, Long Street, Newport (Pembs), Pembrokeshire SA42 0TN. Tel: 01239 820912 Fax: 01239 820912

Milford Haven

94 Charles Street, Milford Haven, Pembrokeshire SA73 2HL. Tel: 01646 690866 Fax: 01646 690655

Pembroke Dock

Irish Ferries, Ferry Terminal, Pembroke Dock, Pembrokeshire SA72 6JZ. Tel: 01646 622753 Fax: 01646 622753

Kilgetty

Kingsmoor Common, Kilgetty, Pembrokeshire SA68 0YA. Tel: 01834 814161 Fax: 01834 814161

St Davids

National Park Visitor Centre, The Grove, St Davids, Pembrokeshire SA62 6NW. Tel: 01437 720392 Fax: 01437 720099

Fishguard

Ocean Lab, The Parrog, Goodwick, Fishguard, Pembrokeshire SA64 0DE. Tel: 01348 872037 Fax: 01348 872528

Haverfordwest

Old Bridge, Haverfordwest, Pembrokeshire SA61 2EZ. Tel: 01437 763110 Fax: 01437 767738

Saundersfoot

The Barbecue, Harbour Car Park, Saundersfoot, Pembrokeshire SA69 9HE. Tel: 01834 813672 Fax: 01834 813673

Tenby

The Croft, Tenby, Pembrokeshire SA70 8AP. Tel: 01834 842402 Fax: 01834 845439

Fishguard

Town Hall, The Square, Fishguard, Pembrokeshire SA65 9HA. Tel: 01348 873484 Fax: 01384 875246

Pembroke

Visitor Centre, Commons Road, Pembroke, Pembrokeshire SA71 4EA. Tel: 01646 622388 Fax: 01646 621396

Carmarthenshire
Carmarthen

113 Lammas Street, Carmarthen, Carmarthenshire SA31 3AQ. Tel: 01267 231557 Fax: 01267 221901

Llandeilo

Car Park, Crescent Road, Llandeilo, Carmarthenshire SA19 6HN. Tel: 01558 824226 Fax: 01558 824226

Llandovery

Heritage Centre, Kings Road, Llandovery, Carmarthenshire SA20 0AW. Tel: 01550 720693 Fax: 01550 720693

Newcastle Emlyn
Market Hall, Newcastle Emlyn, Carmarthenshire SA38 9AE. Tel: 01239 711333 Fax: 01239 711333

Llanarthne
Visitor Information Centre, Llanarthne, Carmarthenshire SA32 3HG. Tel: 01558 669084 Fax: 01558 669084

Swansea Bay
Pont Nedd Fechan
Near Glynneath, Pont Nedd Fechan, Neath & Port Talbot SA11 5NR. Tel: 01639 721795 Fax: 01639 722061

Swansea
Plymouth Street, Swansea, Swansea SA1 3QG. Tel: 01792 468321 Fax: 01792 464602

Mumbles
The Portacabin, Oystermouth Square, Mumbles, Swansea SA3 4DQ. Tel: 01792 361302 Fax: 01792 363392

Isle of Man
Department of Tourism and Leisure, Sea Terminal, Douglas, Isle of Man IM1 2RG. Tel: +44 (0)1624 686801 Fax: +44(0)1624 686800. Email: tourism@gov.im

Channel Islands
Jersey Tourism, Liberation Square, St. Helier JE1 1BB. Tel: 01534 500702

IRELAND – B&B, GUESTHOUSE & FARMSTAY ASSOCIATIONS
Northern Ireland Farm and Country Holidays Association, Greenmount Lodge, 58 Greenmount Road, Omagh, County Tyrone, Northern Ireland BT 79 0YE. Tel: (028) 8284 1325 Fax: (028) 8284 0019.
Email: greenmountlodge@lineone.net Web site: www.nifcha.com

Bed and Breakfast Association Northern Ireland, Aisling House, 7 Taunton Avenue, Belfast, Northern Ireland BT15 4AD. Phone: (028) 9077 1529

Farm Stay UK (formerly the Farm Holiday Bureau), National Agriculture Centre Stoneleigh Park, Warwickshire CV8 2LZ. Tel: (02476) 696909 Fax: (02476) 696630. Website: www.farmstayuk.co.uk Location of properties: UK and Northern Ireland

Irish Farmhouse Holidays Association, Head Office, 2 Michael Street, Limerick. Tel: 00 353(0)61 400700, Fax: 00 353(0)61 400771. Email: farmhols@iol.ie Website: www-irishfarmholidays.com

Town and Country Homes, Belleek Road, Ballyshannon, Co Donegal, Ireland. Tel: 071 98 222 22. Fax: 071 98 222 07. Email: admin@townandcountry.ie. Web site: www.townandcountry.ie WAP: www.bandbireland.com

B&B LISTING AGENCIES

Listed below are some booking agencies, which deal with Bed and Breakfasts.

Academy Travel, POBox 645, London SW16 4SG. Tel: (020) 8679 5738 Fax: (020) 8679 1798. Location of properties: All UK

Always Welcome Homes, 11 Westerdale Road, Greenwich, London SE10 0LW. Tel: (020) 8858 0821 Fax: (020) 8858 7743. Location of properties: All UK

At Home in London, 70 Black Lion Lane, London W6 9BE. Tel: (020) 8748 1943 Fax: (020) 8748 2701. Location of properties: London

Avalon Student Travel, 11 Marlborough Place, Brighton BN1 1UB. Tel: (01273) 243395 Fax: (01273) 243396. Location of properties: All UK

B&B My Guest, 103 Dawes Road, London SW6 7DU. Tel: 0870 444 3840 Fax: 0870 444 3841. Website: www.beduk.co.uk Location of properties: All UK

Bed & Breakfast (GB), 94–96 Bell Street, Henley-on-Thames, Oxfordshire RG9 1XS. Tel: (01491) 578803 Fax: (01491) 410806.

Website: www.bedbreak.com Location of properties: UK

Bed and Breakfast Nationwide, POBox 2100, Clacton on Sea, Essex CO16
9BW. Tel: (01255) 831235 Fax: (01255) 831437.
Website: www.bedandbreakfastnationwide.com Location of properties: UK
and Ireland

The Brackett Agency, Brockhillburn, Ettrickbridge, Selkirk TD7 5JH. Tel:
(01750) 52210 Fax: (01750) 52210. Location of properties: Edinburgh

Centa UK Ltd, Foresters, 31 Chapel Street, Cam, Dursley, Gloucester GL11
5NY. Tel: (01453) 548200/(01453) 549996 Fax: (01453) 548200. Mobile: 0973
890477. Website: www.centauk.co.uk Location of properties: Cotswolds,
Yorkshire Dales and Moors

Distinctly Different, Bradford Old Windmill, 4 Masons Lane, Bradford-on-Avon
Wiltshire BA15 1QN. Tel: (01225) 866648 Fax: (01225) 866648. Location of
properties: England, Wales and Scotland

En Famille Agency (Britain), Suite 16, Gerrard House Business Centre,
Worthing Road, East Preston, West Sussex BN16 1AW. Tel: (01903) 783636
Fax: (01903) 783630. Location of properties: All Britain

English Host Holidays, 21 Manor Way, Hayling Island, Hampshire PO11 9JH
Tel: (01705) 462191 Fax: (01705) 468227. Location of properties: Southern
England

Euro-Academy Ltd, 77a George Street, Croydon, Surrey CR0 1LD. Tel: (020)
8681 2905 Fax: (020) 8681 8850. Location of properties: All UK

Euroyouth Ltd, 301 Westborough Road, Southend-on-Sea (Westcliff), Essex
SS0 9PT. Tel: (01702) 341434 Fax: (01702) 330104. Location of properties:
Mostly Southend-on-Sea, some London suburbs

Families in Britain, Martins Cottage, Martins Lane, Birdham, Chichester
Sussex PO20 7AU. Tel: (01243) 512222 Fax: (01243) 511377. Location of
properties: UK

Festival Beds, 38 Moray Place, Edinburgh EH3 6BT. Tel: (0131) 225 1101 Fax: (0131) 623 7123. Location of properties: Edinburgh city centre

FERN (Franco European Relations Negotiators), 105 Gordon Road, Camberley Surrey GU15 2JQ. Tel: (01276) 27033 Fax: (01276) 27033. Location of properties: Outer London, Surrey, Hampshire, Berkshire

Happy Homes, Beaufort Street, Chelsea, London SW3. Tel: (020) 7352 5121 Fax: (020) 7352 5121. Website: www.happy-homes.com Location of properties: Predominantly central London, especially south-west

Holiday Hosts, 59 Cromwell Road, London SW19 8LF. Tel: (020) 8540 7942 Fax: (020) 8540 2827. Location of properties: South and west London

Home from Home Accommodation Service, The Old Granary, Fillongley, Nr Coventry CV7 8PB. Tel: (01676) 541896 Fax: (01203) 256825. Location of properties: Throughout England

Homes Away, 3 Aldham Hall, New Wanstead, London E11 2SQ. Tel: (020) 8530 2271 Fax: (020) 8530 2271. Location of properties: Quiet residential areas. Woodford, South Woodford, Wanstead and east London

Host and Guest Service, 103 Dawes Road, London SW6 7DU. Tel: (020) 7385 9922 Fax: (020) 7386 7575. Website: www.host-guest.co.uk Location of properties: Throughout the country, especially London

Jolaine Agency, 18 Escot Way, Barnet, Hertfordshire EN5 3AN. Tel: (020) 8449 1334 Fax: (020) 8449 9183. Location of properties: Mainly north-west London suburbs – other areas on request

Knights in Britain, Arundell House, High Street, Tisbury, Wiltshire SP3 6PS. Tel: (01747) 871221 Fax: (01747) 871281. Location of properties: All UK

The London Bed & Breakfast Agency Limited, 71 Fellows Road, London NW3 3JY. Tel: (020) 7586 2768 Fax: (020) 7586 6567. Location of properties:

North, south, south-west and west London

London First Choice Accommodation, 111 Hill Rise, Greenford UB6 8PE. Tel: (020) 8575 8877 Fax: (020) 8575 8877. Location of properties: Central London and suburbs

London Homestead Services, Coombe Wood Road, Kingston Upon Thames, Surrey KT2 7JY. Tel: (020) 8949 4455 Fax: (020) 8549 5492. Location of properties: London

Mondial Agency, 32 Links Road, West Wickham, Kent BR4 0QW. Tel: (020) 8777 6271 Fax: (020) 8777 6765. Location of properties: UK

New East International Ltd, PO Box 292, Pinner HA5 1UF. Tel: (020) 8933 1460 Fax: (020) 8866 5520. Location of properties: UK

Norfolk and Suffolk Farm Holiday Group, Monterey, Lodge Close, Thurston, Bury St Edmunds, Suffolk IP31 3RS. Tel/Fax: (01359) 231013. Website: www.farmstayanglia.co.uk Location of properties: Norfolk and Suffolk

Overseas Visitor Service (OVS), 192 Brighton Road, Lancing, West Sussex BN15 8LJ. Tel: (01903) 762097 Fax: (01273) 453143. Location of properties: Lancing and Worthing, West Sussex

Peaceful Holidays Ltd, 97 Fieldhead Rd, Guiseley, Leeds LS20 8DU. Tel: (01943) 872765 Fax: (01973) 872765. Location of properties: Yorkshire Dales and Moors

The Primrose Hill Agency for Bed and Breakfast, 14 Edis Street, London NW1 8LG. Tel: (020) 7722 6869 Fax: (020) 7916 2240. Location of properties: North London – Hampstead, Highgate, Primrose Hill

Thameside Homestay, 120 Thurleston Avenue, Morden, Surrey SM4 4EG. Tel: (020) 8395 0389 Fax: (020) 8395 0389. Location of properties: All UK

Uptown Reservations, 50 Christchurch Street, Chelsea, London SW3 4AR. Tel: (020) 7351 3445 Fax: (020) 7351 9383. Location of properties: Kensington, Chelsea, Knightsbridge, Belgravia, Holland Park, Parsons Green, Notting Hill

Welcome Homes and Hotels, 21 Kellerton Road, London SE13 5RB. Tel: (020) 8265 1212 Fax: (020) 8852 3243. Website: www.welcomehomes.co.uk Location of properties: All UK

Wolsey Lodges, 9 Market Place, Hadleigh, Ipswich, Suffolk IP7 5DL. Tel: (01473) 822058 Fax: (01473) 827444. Website: www.wolsey-lodges.co.uk Location of properties: All UK

ALCOHOL LICENCES
Here are the contact details of two legal firms who can assist you in securing the appropriate alcohol licence for your establishment.

Republic of Ireland
William Fry, Solicitors, Fitzwilton House, Wilton Place, Dublin 2, Ireland. Tel: +353 1 639 5000 Fax: +353 1 639 5333. Direct Dial: +353 1 639 5367 Web site: www.williamfry.ie/licencinglaw.html

England
Fisher Jones Greenwood, Norfolk House, Southway, Colchester, Essex CO2 7BA. Tel: +44 (0)1206 578282 Fax: +44 (0)1206 760282. DX: 3600 Colchester Web site: www.lawcentre.co.uk

Business name registration
For businesses in England or Wales
Business Names Section, Companies House, Crown Way, Cardiff CF14 3UZ. Tel: (029) 2038 0362

For businesses in Scotland
The Registrar of Companies, Companies House, 37 Castle Terrace,

Edinburgh EH1 2EB. Tel: (0131) 535 5800

For businesses in Ireland

Companies Registration Office, Parnell House, 14 Parnell Square, Dublin 1, Ireland. Tel: (01804) 5200

For businesses in Northern Ireland

Companies Registry, IDB House, 64 Chichester Street, Belfast BT1 4JX. Tel: (028) 9054 4888/4999

ENERGY EFFICIENCY

There are many Energy Efficiency Advice Centres (EEACs) across the UK who give advice to people in their locality. We suggest you call the national EEAC free-phone number: 0800 512 012.

You may also wish to contact the Carbon Trust, a sister organisation at: www.thecarbontrust.co.uk

BED SUPPLIER

Sealy United Kingdom, Station Road, Aspatria, Carlisle, Cumbria, England CA5 2AS. Tel: 016973 20342 for both the UK and Ireland.

HOME RENOVATION INTERNET SITES

The following are some helpful Internet sites on house renovation tips and ideas.

www.thisoldhouse.com
www.oldhouses.com.au

OTHER WEB SITES

www.bnb-central.com. This the author's web site for updated contact points for your consideration.

www.howtobooks.co.uk This web site is ideal for those seeking other 'how to books' on a multitude of subjects.

PRE-PAID VOUCHERS

Discover Travel & Tours PLC, International House, Pierpoint Street, Worcester WR1 1YD. Tel: +44 (0) 870 225 8000 www.discovertravelandtours.com

Index